THE EVERYTHING®
EASY LARGE-PRINT WORD SEARCH BOOK, VOLUME 2

Dear Reader,

Easy does it. That's my motto when it comes to puzzles. These word search puzzles are easy—that's what makes them so much fun. They will engage your brain without melting it down! With a gentle focus, words will appear in what seem like random letters. With enough concentration, even the last word will be revealed. You will return to the real world triumphant and refreshed.

It was a pleasure creating these puzzles for you. I've given each one a theme to make the solving more interesting. The grids have been loaded with relevant words. We used large print because bigger letters are better; finding the words is less tedious. Puzzles that are easy on the eyes are more fun for the brain.

So find a comfy chair and grab a pen or pencil. Get ready for a pleasant journey through these pages. Your brain will thank you for this relaxing diversion. Let's take it easy!

Charles Timmerman

Welcome to the EVERYTHING. Series!

These handy, accessible books give you all you need to tackle a difficult project, gain a new hobby, comprehend a fascinating topic, prepare for an exam, or even brush up on something you learned back in school but have since forgotten.

You can choose to read an Everything® book from cover to cover or just pick out the information you want from our four useful boxes: e-questions, e-facts, e-alerts, and e-ssentials. We give you everything you need to know on the subject, but throw in a lot of fun stuff along the way, too.

We now have more than 400 Everything® books in print, spanning such wide-ranging categories as weddings, pregnancy, cooking, music instruction, foreign language, crafts, pets, New Age, and so much more. When you're done reading them all, you can finally say you know Everything®!

PUBLISHER Karen Cooper

MANAGING EDITOR, EVERYTHING® SERIES Lisa Laing

COPY CHIEF Casey Ebert

ASSISTANT PRODUCTION EDITOR Melanie Cordova

ACQUISITIONS EDITOR Lisa Laing

EDITORIAL ASSISTANT Matthew Kane

EVERYTHING® SERIES COVER DESIGNER Erin Alexander

LAYOUT DESIGNERS Erin Dawson, Michelle Roy Kelly, Elisabeth Lariviere

Visit the entire Everything® series at *www.everything.com*

THE

EVERYTHING
EASY
LARGE-PRINT
WORD SEARCH
BOOK
VOLUME 2

150 large-print easy word search puzzles

Charles Timmerman
Founder of Funster.com

Adams Media
New York London Toronto Sydney New Delhi

Adams Media
An Imprint of Simon & Schuster, Inc.
100 Technology Center Drive
Stoughton, MA 02072

An Everything® Series Book.
Everything® and everything.com® are registered trademarks of Simon & Schuster, Inc.

ADAMS MEDIA and colophon are trademarks of Simon and Schuster.

For information about special discounts for bulk purchases, please contact Simon & Schuster Special Sales at 1-866-506-1949 or business@simonandschuster.com.

The Simon & Schuster Speakers Bureau can bring authors to your live event. For more information or to book an event contact the Simon & Schuster Speakers Bureau at 1-866-248-3049 or visit our website at www.simonspeakers.com.

Manufactured in the United States of America

17 2023

ISBN 978-1-4405-3889-6

Acknowledgments

I would like to thank each and every one of the more than half a million people who have visited my website, *www.funster.com*, to play word games and puzzles. You have shown me how much fun puzzles can be and how addictive they can become!

It is a pleasure to acknowledge the folks at Adams Media who made this book possible. I particularly want to thank my editor, Lisa Laing, for so skillfully managing the many projects we have worked on together.

Contents

Introduction

The puzzles in this book are in the traditional word search format. Words in the list are hidden in the puzzle in any direction: up, down, forward, backward, or diagonally. The words are always found in a straight line and letters are never skipped. Words can overlap. For example, the two letters at the end of the word "MAST" could be used as the start of the word "STERN." Only uppercased letters are used, and any spaces in an entry are removed. For example, "TROPICAL FISH" would be found in the puzzle as "TROPICALFISH." Apostrophes and hyphens are also omitted in the puzzles. Draw a circle around each word that you find. Then cross the word off the list so that you will always know which words remain to be found.

A favorite strategy is to look for the first letter in a word, then see if the second letter is in any of the neighboring letters, and so on until the word is found. Or instead of searching for the first letter in a word, it is sometimes easier to look for letters that stand out, like Q, U, X, and Z. Double letters in a word will also stand out and be easier to find. Another strategy is to simply scan each row, column, and diagonal looking for any words.

Puzzles

ACCURACY

AIM

AMERICAN

ARROWS

BAR

BEER

BULLS EYE

CIRCULAR

COMPETITIONS

CRICKET

DARTBOARD

DOUBLING OUT

DRINKING

ERIC BRISTOW

FIVES

HITS

INNER BULL

IRIS

JUMPERS

LEG

NODOR

OCHE

OUTER BULL

PHIL TAYLOR

PLAYERS

PUB GAME

SPORT

STANDARDIZED

TARGET

TED HANKEY

THROWING

TOURNAMENTS

TRINA GULLIVER

UNITED KINGDOM

WALL

```
I P B B D A R T B O A R D S
T D E Z I D R A D N A T S W
O R R Y T H R O W I N G E O
U N I T E D K I N G D O M R
R Y C N T S R E P M U J A R
N C B A A I L O H D S T G A
A A R C R G C L M O T E B L
M R I I G H U I U U I D U U
E U S R E Y A L P B H H P C
N C T E T Q B H L L B A R R
T C O M P E T I T I O N S I
S A W A E R O D O N V K P C
E I D R I N K I N G W E O K
V L L U B R E T U O A Y R E
I B E I N N E R B U L L T T
F Y A G R O L Y A T L I H P
```

Solution on Page 314

ASIA	QUALITY
BLOUSE	ROBE
CHINESE	SATIN
CLOTHING	SCARF
COCOONS	SHEETS
DRESS	SHIMMER
DYED	SKIRT
FABRIC	SMOOTH
FASHION	SOFT
FIBERS	SPIDER
INSECTS	STRONG
JAPAN	SUIT
KIMONO	TEXTURE
LARVAE	THREAD
LIGHT	TIES
LINGERIE	TRADE
LUXURY	WEAVING
MATERIAL	WOVEN
MULBERRY	
PATTERN	
POPULAR	
PROTEIN	

```
L I G H T O O M S S E R D R
S K I R T F D P V T D K A E
T B M T E X T U R E E C E D
R L Q U A L I T Y O L E R I
A O A A L L U D F O T S H P
D U I I S B S R T O L E T S
E S I Q R H E H G P S N I G
A E N N E E I R E G N I L N
B A E R S N T M R P F H S I
J V V E G E G A M Y A C T V
A R O T L F C X M E B O R A
P A W T U S A T I N R C O E
A L Q A X X F A S H I O N W
N P O P U L A R H O C O G R
G S C A R F E K I M O N O S
P T M B Y D F I B E R S S N
```

Solution on Page 314

BARREN	MOOSE
BIRDS	NATURE
BOOTS	OUTDOORS
BRIGHT	PARK
CABIN	PEOPLE
CALM	POND
CHILLY	QUIET
COAT	RABBITS
COLD	RANGER
CRUNCHY	SCARF
DECEMBER	SERENE
DORMANT	SILENCE
DRIFTS	SLEIGH
ELK	VALLEY
EMPTY	WEATHER
FIR TREE	WHITE
FOREST	WIND
FROZEN	WOODS
GLOVES	
HOLLY	
ICICLES	
LIGHTS	

Solution on

```
H S C A U F R A C S W D S D
B D R Y B B I R D S R N E B
U O U T D O O R S T E I U Q
Z O N P N E Y Y T E B W C S
Z W C M K S L D O R M A N T
P D H E R L L K O U E S U I
U N Y F O E I T B T C E V B
O O D H I I H C J A E L A B
M P N R W G C T C N D C L A
H L A H I H V T A N Y I L R
Q S I R P F S I L E N C E R
J T B M K E T G M R W I Y A
E H A O R L O S F R O Z E N
T G L O V E S P C A B I N G
M I F S C O L D L B X E Z E
S L M E E E N E R E S E H R
```

Solution on Page 314

ABSTRACT	MINIMALISM
AMERICAN	MONUMENT
ANIMALIERS	MOUNTAIN
ART	PORTRAITS
BRONZE	REALISM
BUILDINGS	REMINGTON
CERAMIC	ROMANTIC
CLAY	RUSHMORE
COMMISSION	SCULPTOR
CRAFT	SHOW
CULTURE	STATUE
DECORATION	TOOLS
FOLK	TOYS
FURNITURE	WILDLIFE
GALLERY	WOOD
HOMEGROWN	
HONOR	
LANDSCAPE	
LIBERTY	
LINCOLN	
MEMORIAL	
METAL	

```
R D E N W O R G E M O H K D
O E E P O R T R A I T S I O
T Z A C M O U N T A I N S O
P N C L O T C A R T S B A W
L O W L I R E M I N G T O N
U R S N A S A H N E A H C M
C B R P K Y M T O N S A E O
S U M S I L A M I N I M R N
F I C L A T E M S O O E A U
G L U E U T A T S R N R M M
A D L W I L D L I F E I I E
L I T C I T N A M O R C C N
L N U E F O L K M C R A F T
E G R R U S H M O R E N G O
R S E L A N D S C A P E O Y
Y T R E B I L I N C O L N S
```

Solution on Page 314

ALLERGIES

ANIMALS

APRIL

AUTUMN

BIRTH

BLOOMING

BLOSSOM

CLIMATE

COLORFUL

CROCUSES

DAFFODILS

EARTH

EASTER

EQUINOX

FALL

FESTIVALS

FLOWERS

GRASS

GREEN

GROWTH

HOT

KITE

LEAVES

LENT

MARCH

MAY DAY

MELT

NATURE

NEW LIFE

PLANTS

RAIN

RENEWAL

SEASON

SUMMER

SUNSHINE

THAW

TULIPS

WARMTH

WEATHER

WINTER

```
H W A H T O H L B I R T H G
T S I X R S E L E A V E S R
M U A N E N O S A E S V F A
R M U G T S E F I L W E N S
A M T R S E E N I H S N U S
W E U O A I R N A T U R E N
K R M W E G G N I M O O L B
I E N T E R W V T U L I P S
T H Y H P E A Z C G R E E N
E T A M I L C P O M A R C H
Q A D E S L L S L A M I N A
U E Y A D A F F O D I L S A
I W A R N L D S R E W O L F
N O M T L E M Y F R A I N A
O S S H D S E S U C O R C L
X A R E N E W A L I R P A L
```

Solution on Page 315

ADULT	MATE
BABIES	MOTHER
BEES	ONLY ONE
BOSS	PHEROMONE
BREED	PIPING
BUZZ	PROTECTED
COLONY	QUEEN CUPS
COMB	REPRODUCE
DIES	ROYAL
DOMINANT	RULER
DRONE	SIZE
EGG	SPECIAL
FEMALE	STATUS
FERTILIZE	STING
FIGHTING	VIRGIN
FLY	WAX
HIVE	WING
HONEY	YELLOW
JELLY	
KEEPER	
LARGE	
LEADER	

```
F L M M E B W W K D I E S M
W R E X O H I V E R E L U R
M M C S Z T S P E C I A L R
F T S O R B H P P I P I N G
I A D U L T R E E B E D Y N
G S L A Y O R X R N E Z I S
H E P E D L N P O E D E U Z
T E N U L M F Y R E D T S W
I N C O C A L B T G A A I O
N E A B M N M C S T E N E L
G V U N O O E E S W G Y G L
E Z I L I T R E F D R O N E
Z G E R O M I E U H A M I Y
V L G R G B O H H Q L A T X
M X P F A I B D P P X T S A
C O M B H O N E Y L L E J W
```

Solution on Page 315

AIR

BABIES

BALLOON

BIRDS

BREAD

BUBBLE

BUTTON

CLOUDS

CORK

COTTON

DUST

FEATHER

FLOWER

FLUFF

FOAM

GAUZE

GLOVES

GRASS

HELIUM

INSECT

KITE

KLEENEX

LEAF

LINT

MAKEUP

NAPKIN

PEN

PILLOW

PUPPY

SAND

SATIN

SEED

SILK

SMOKE

SOCKS

STEAM

STRAW

THREAD

TISSUE

VAPOR

```
W P E P U E K A M P B B H X
A F B S O C K S B U U W C K
B E N Y I Q E A B T I O R I
M A E T S V B B T S I L K F
U T L H O I L O R I A L E W
W H K L E E N E X O I I W H
Q E G S O C K U Z Y P P U P
B R D C L O U D S U S A N D
F T O B M T N I K P A N V V
B R C S F T H R E A D G Q I
K X R E W O L F F U L F N D
R D E E S N A M R C Z G B U
C V T A D N K M S W A R T S
P O T N R T I S S U E A R T
E I E T I K U L E A F S C B
N D C P B L X E D L B S Z C
```

Solution on Page 315

ALCOHOL

ANTIBIOTIC

ASPIRIN

BANDAGES

BLANKET

BLEEDING

BLOOD

BOX

BURNS

CAMPING

CARE

CLEAN

CREAM

CUT

EMERGENCY

GAUZE

GLOVES

HEALTH

HELP

HOME

HOSPITAL

IODINE

LIFE

MASK

MEDICINE

OINTMENTS

RED CROSS

SAFETY

SALINE

SAVING

SCISSORS

SPLINTS

STERILE

SUPPLIES

SURVIVAL

SWABS

TWEEZERS

WORK

WOUNDS

WRAP

```
U S D N U O W O R K L V D B
G A U Z E I C P A R W I H A
G L O V E S R S W A B S F T
N I E L I R E T S L E S S E
I N A M C O A N E C M T U K
V E F N A S M E R O O N R N
A Y T M T S D M E H H I V A
S T W U U I K T D O E L I L
N E E P N C B N C L L P V B
R F E G A S N I R I P S A I
U A Z N E B L O O D E N L O
B S E I L P P U S T D J J D
O E R P C U T H S A I P Z I
X E S M E M E R G E N C Y N
H T L A E H M E D I C I N E
E R A C H O S P I T A L O F
```

Solution on Page 315

ALPHABET

ART

AUTHOR

BIBLE

BLOCK

BOOK

CLOTH

COPY

DESIGN

DEVICE

EDIT

FAST

FONT

FORME

FRISKET

GUTENBERG

INK

JOURNALISM

KNOWLEDGE

LEAD

LETTER

LITERACY

MASS

MECHANICAL

MODERN

MOVABLE

NEWS

PAGES

PAPER

PLATE

PRESSURE

PUBLISH

ROLL

SPEED

SURFACE

TEXT

TRANSFER

TYMPAN

TYPE

WORDS

```
C X W N D N I L G M B P G T
W L J Y U E G D E L W O N K
O X O O Z T R A N S F E R O
R O H T U A E R K C O L B O
D D X F H R B T F O N T I B
S M E C H A N I C A L E B S
X S O E U O E A L D S X L P
H P A W P C T L L E T T E R
Y S S M I S U P O I I I Y F
T Y I V T P G H R D S C T O
Y E E L A Y D A E L A M Y R
M D O G B H P B N R E D O M
P R E S S U R E E P L A T E
A S R E P A P T E K S I R F
N W T D E S I G N E W S N E
M O V A B L E C A F R U S K
```

Solution on Page 316

ALGAE	LATIN
ANIMAL	LIFE
ARCHAEA	MONERA
BACTERIA	ORDER
BIOLOGY	ORGANISM
BOTANY	ORIGIN
CATEGORIES	PHYLA
CELL	PLANT
CHROMISTA	PROTISTA
CLASS	RANK
DIVIDED	RESEARCH
DIVISION	SCIENCE
DOMAIN	SPECIES
EMPIRES	SYSTEM
EVOLUTION	TAXONOMY
FAMILY	TREE
FUNGI	ZOOLOGY
GENUS	
GROUP	
HIERARCHY	
HISTORY	
KINGDOM	

```
C H R O M I S T A R E N O M
A E F I L L E C N E I C S D
T Q N Q P H Y L A M I N A P
E V O L U T I O N S U N E G
G S I B A C T E R I A C K B
O P S Y S T E M R N G S N I
R E I F A M I L Y A G I A O
I C V O H C K N M G R H R L
E I I A T S I T O R P C C O
S E D N B A M Y N O H R H G
H S A E M O G R O U C A A Y
I L W O D O U O X P L E E N
P G D G L I R T A T A S A A
S L N O Z D V S T R S E G T
Y I O U E M P I R E S R L O
K Z H R F R A H D E J M A B
```

Solution on Page 316

ANCHOR	LEAD
ANVIL	LOGS
BED	LUGGAGE
BOATS	METAL
BOULDER	PIANO
BOXES	PLANES
BRICK	RHINO
BUS	SHIP
CAR	SOFA
CEMENT	STEEL
COAT	STOVE
CONCRETE	TABLE
COUCH	TANKS
DESKS	TIRES
ELEPHANT	TRAIN
FORKLIFT	TRUCK
FRIDGE	WASHER
GOLD	WHALE
GUILT	
HEART	
HORSES	
IRON	

```
U Y K C U R T U J R C B P B
C T F L K N I A R T O I O P
S T O V E I R S O F A A A L
U G R A L C E M E N T N U A
S S K S E D S T O S C G A N
I G L T R A E H O H G N L E
G U I L T R C H O A V Y A S
O V F J C U S R G I K V L T
L R T N A H P E L E C B N E
D A O S C W G D X B I O E E
E C L E A D L L P O R K C L
B S A S I S J U A I B B K A
G K W R H C U O C T H U V H
V N F O E E L B A T E S S W
W A S H E R H I N O J M E T
M T N L V P S H L O X L I U
```

Solution on Page 316

ANIMAL

BALD

BEAK

BIRD OF PREY

BROWN

CHICKS

DDT

DIET

EAGLES

EGGS

EMBLEM

ENDANGERED

FEATHERS

FISH

FLIGHT

FLYING

FREE

GREAT SEAL

HABITAT

HUNT

LARGE

NESTING

PLUMAGE

POWERFUL

PREDATOR

PROTECTED

QUARTER

RAPTOR

RARE

REGAL

SKY

SOAR

SPECIES PAIR

SYMBOL

TALONS

TREE

USA

WHITE HEAD

WILDLIFE

WINGSPAN

```
Z E G G S E L G A E G R A L
H U N T P M E R A R E G A L
E C A D E R E G N A D N E B
E R P P C H I C K S I Y A R
R A S L I M E L B M E L E O
T P G U E E R F A R D T Q W
P T N M S D K L P D R T M N
K O I A P U E F B A D H F R
X R W G A S O T U E D G E O
O G K E I D N Q C H T I A T
H T A G R E A T S E A L T A
R A E I S F T S I T T F H D
A L B T H W U D U I I O E E
O O I G N I Y L F H B Y R R
S N E F I L D L I W A E S P
G S K Y L O B M Y S H S I F
```

Solution on Page 316

BIG

BROAD

CHUBBY

CIRCLE

COLOSSAL

CROOKED

CURVED

DEEP

DIAMOND

ELLIPSE

FAT

FLAT

GREAT

HEXAGON

HIGH

HOLLOW

HUGE

IMMENSE

JUMBO

LARGE

LITTLE

MAMMOTH

MASSIVE

NARROW

OCTAGON

OVAL

PETITE

PUNY

ROUND

SCRAWNY

SHALLOW

SHORT

SKINNY

SMALL

SQUARE

STAR

STEEP

TALL

TINY

WIDE

```
P I N H U G E L W Y N E B O U
U G L H N D L L O O J C E I
N E G R E A T S T A R I G W
Y I E X M O P E E T S R R Q
H N Y S C R A W N Y I C A X
O O N H P B P S G L I L L N
O C E I D I M M E N S E M P
S N R R K I L F S Q U A R E
C O L O S S A L O B M U J E
M G F U O O H M E M N H D D
K A A N O K C A O S H O R T
T X S D W H E T L N F L O L
U E G S U W H D A L D L V L
T H I B I D E A I G O O A A
R T B D E V R U C W O W L T
J Y E T I T E P Q T I N Y Q
```

Solution on Page 317

APRIL	HUNT
BASKET	JELLY BEANS
BONNET	KIDS
BUNNY	MYTH
CHILD	PASTELS
CHURCH	PRETEND
COSTUME	RABBIT
CUTE	SPRING
DYE	SUNDAY
EARS	SURPRISE
EASTER	SYMBOL
EGG	TAIL
FAMILY	TOY
FLOWERS	TRADITION
FOLKLORE	TREATS
FUN	WHITE
GAMES	
GIFTS	
GRASS	
HARE	
HIDE	
HOP	

```
D Y Y I K B I J O L K F M F
R D S G G E T U C E I F V J
R H L F A M I L Y A D N U S
K I E S F L O W E R S S L N
L D T R A D I T I O N I E W
I E S G A K T E K S A B N M
R R A Y W B D N E T E R P K
P A P Y Y H B G U M B Y F Q
A H O L N H I I U H Y O D Z
S T B O N N E T T D L I H C
E Y S B U P S Q E K L O L G
Q M S M B O E Z L L E O N I
U H A Y C H A O C A J I C F
K X R S H C R U H C R X N T
U X G A M E S I R P R U S S
K L T T R E A T S Q E Z K P
```

Solution on Page 317

AGE

ALCOHOL

BLANC

BOTTLE

BRUT

BUBBLY

CELLAR

CHEERS

CLEAR

CORK

CRISTAL

DATE

DRY

FANCY

FERMENT

FESTIVE

FINE

FLUTE

FRANCE

GLASS

GRAPES

ICE

ITALY

LABEL

LIQUID

LOVE

LUXURY

MIMOSA

PARTY

PINK

POP

QUALITY

RED

ROSE

SWEET

TIPSY

TOAST

VINE

WHITE

WINE

```
M Y K X A B D E R T O A S T
I C E S Y A Q Y E T I H W W
E N P R T T T R M S E P O P
G A D E S E K U I Q O E S L
K F Z E E I E X M U G R W Y
H R R H A V I U O A R R E A
P A L C O H O L S L A L E H
P N F L U T E K A I P I T R
L C L E A R N V X T E Q N A
R E A N B I Z Z I Y S U E L
G N B I P A R T Y T C I M L
D I E V S S A L G I S D R E
P W L N J P B O T T L E E C
X M K L I B L A N C U S F Q
G J I J U F L P T S K R O C
X Z F B D Y U D K U C J B F
```

Solution on Page 317

ALL

BELL

BULL

CELL

COAL

COOL

DEAL

DIAL

DOLL

DULL

EVIL

FAIL

FEEL

FELL

FOOL

FOUL

FUEL

FULL

GIRL

GOAL

GULL

HAIL

HAUL

HEEL

HELL

ILL

JAIL

MAIL

MEAL

NAIL

OIL

ORAL

OVAL

OWL

PAIL

PEEL

POOL

PULL

RAIL

REAL

```
F G I R L F D A L D N F E U
L A V A I K O O X U E V E L
Q L I J A R O O L L I F L A
I D E L J C V F L L E U F E
C I E H O R E A A W G L S M
G E Q A A E Q M R L F L M I
Q Y L I L L L I O D O A I S
U Z L L U B E J B V I O B R
K C L O A W C E H L A G P S
D E F I H E Q P H I P L E G
B R H A O I Z E L A E R H H
R Z C H Q W V E I N A E D A
J K T S H I L L B Q O V R W
R B I T Q K L Y S Y P B M S
S Z U N K U P M O X C N A E
M E Z K P Z L W B Y F N R V
```

Solution on Page 317

ACTIVITIES	HELP
ADULTS	JOIN
ASSOCIATION	KIDS
BASKETBALL	LEAGUES
BODY	LOCAL
BOYS	MEMBERSHIP
BUILDING	MIND
CAMPING	MOVEMENT
CENTER	NONPROFIT
CHILDREN	POOLS
CHRISTIAN	PROGRAMS
CLASSES	SPIRIT
CLUB	SPORTS
COMMUNITY	THEY
DIRECTOR	VOLUNTEER
EXERCISE	YOUNG MEN
FAMILY	YWCA
FITNESS	
FUN	
GIRLS	
GROUP	
HEALTHY	

```
Y B P L T M D I R E C T O R
O L C S H E A L T H Y W C A
U A A P E M B A I B O Y S H
N C M I Y B O L E A G U E S
G O P R M E D J X S C F S Y
M L I I I R Y O E K E E Y T
E A N T E S T I R E N S L I
N D G N A H T N C T T M I N
B U I L D I N G I B E A M U
S L F F V P C F S A R R A M
E T K I D S O O E L G G F M
S S T S T R O P S L O O P O
S C A U P N A I T S I R H C
A O T N E M E V O M A P E L
L V O L U N T E E R Q Z L U
C N P U O R G I R L S K P B
```

Solution on Page 318

AFRICAN BUSH

AFRICAN FOREST

ASIAN ELEPHANT

BABY

BIG

CALVES

CIRCUS

DUMBO

EARS

ELEPHANTIDAE

ENDANGERED

FEET

GRASSLANDS

HANNIBAL

HEAVY

INTELLIGENCE

IVORY

JUMBO

LOXODONTA

MAMMALS

MAMMOTHS

MEMORY

PACHYDERM

POACHERS

PROBOSCIDEA

SAFARI

SIZE

SKIN

SMART

TAIL

TEETH

TRUMPET

TRUNKS

TUSKS

WALK

WATER

WILDLIFE

```
S R E H C A O P W W L S Q S
E L E P H A N T I D A E R K
C I T O E F Y M L U B V D N
N H U B A R R A D M I L E U
E R S M V I O M L B N A R R
G E K U Y C V M I O N C E T
I T S J B A I A F G A S G A
L A S I A N E L E P H A N T
L W G G B F A S I X T F A N
E P R O B O S C I D E A D O
T Y S U C R I C I A E R N D
N R R I T E P M U R T I E O
I O A T N S M A R T F A Z X
K M E S H T O M M A M A I O
S E S D N A L S S A R G S L
F M R E D Y H C A P K L A W
```

Solution on Page 318

ASTROLABE

COMETS

CONSTELLATIONS

DARK

DIGITAL

DISPLAY

DOMES

EARTH

EDUCATIONAL

ENTERTAINING

HEAVENS

LASERS

MILKY WAY

MODEL

MOON

MUSEUMS

NIGHT SKY

OBSERVATORY

ORRERY

PLANETARIUM

PRESENTATION

PROJECTORS

ROOM

SCIENCE

SHOWS

SIMULATION

SOLAR SYSTEM

SPACE

STARS

SUN

TECHNOLOGY

THEATERS

UNIVERSE

ZEISS

```
G S S M U E S U M S W O H S
L N S T E C H N O L O G Y P
A O I U S T E M O C N P E R
T I E N N O S S N I R L D O
I T Z P I I R Y G E A E U J
G A Y C L A V H S S H D C E
I L A R T A T E E R X O A C
D L W S O S N R R A A M T T
L E Y C K T S E E S V L I O
S T K Y A R A Y T T E E O R
C S L T O O A V R A N U N S
I N I O E L E D R E R E A S
E O M S P A C E I E R I L R
N C U S R B D O M E S R U B
C N I T H E A T E R S B O M
E D H F S I M U L A T I O N
```

Solution on Page 318

ADVERTISING

ARTICLES

AUDIENCE

BIAS

BLOGS

BOOKS

CABLE

COMMERCIAL

COMPUTER

DOCUMENT

ELECTRONIC

FACTS

FILMS

INFORMATION

INTERNET

JOURNALIST

LARGE

MAGAZINES

MARKETING

MEDIA

MOVIES

MUSIC

NEWSPAPERS

PAPARAZZI

PODCAST

POLITICS

PRESS

PROGRAMMING

PROPAGANDA

RADIO

TELEVISION

VIDEO

WEB

WRITER

```
C I S U M D O C U M E N T T
C M A G A Z I N E S L G S S
A A M D P M E D I A N P I A
B R O M V C M M I I L F L C
L K V I D E O C M B K Y A D
E E I N F O R M A T I O N O
C T E F P E A T P S S E R P
N I S E M R E R I U W F U O
E N N M G N O Z T S T F O L
I G O O R R Z P P I I E J I
D C R E R A A A A L C N R T
U P T A R T P L M G P L G I
A N D A Q E C S T C A F E C
I I P W R I T E R A Z N P S
O A E S K O O B L O G S D U
P B G N O I S I V E L E T A
```

Solution on Page 318

ALUMNI	PAST
AUTUMN	PEP
BALL	PICNIC
BAND	PRINCE
BONFIRE	PROM
COLLEGE	QUEEN
COURT	RALLY
CROWN	RETURN
CULTURE	REUNION
DANCE	ROYALTY
DATE	SCHEDULE
DRESS	SCHOOL
EVENT	SPORTS
FALL	STUDENTS
FLOAT	TAILGATE
FORMAL	TICKETS
FRIENDS	WEEKEND
GAME	WELCOME
KING	
MUSIC	
OCCASION	
PARTY	

```
J B W O H J E Y N W F E Z K
P A W E L C O M E Y O Z I V
R N W O R C U E E N R N X Q
I D A N I T K Y U R M Y L Y
N O I N U E R T Q U A T L R
C S C A N R T R L T L L A J
E I C D P I K A F E A A F S
P O S H R F F P G R N Y V F
S E C U O N A Z G L O O C Q
S T G U M O S D N E I R F O
E E U E L B L L A B S A E G
R T M D L T R U O C A T T N
D A N C E L U D E H C S A I
G O I J J N O R S E C A D K
N L E V E N T C E G O P E P
E F S T R O P S T E K C I T
```

Solution on Page 319

ACETIC

ACID

AGED

APPLE

AROMA

BALSAMIC

BITTER

BOTTLE

CHIPS

CLEAN

COCONUT

CONDIMENT

COOKING

DISTILLED

DOMESTIC

ETHANOL

FERMENTED

FLAVOR

FOOD

FRUIT

INDUSTRIAL

KITCHEN

LIQUID

MALT

MARINADES

MEDICAL

MOTHER

OIL

PICKLE

RED

RICE

SALT

SHERRY

SMELL

SOUR

TART

TASTE

WATER

WHITE

WINE

```
S F T R A T L A M Z E E W B
G O R T A S T E G M N C M K
P O U E L P P A C E T I C A
A D M R D W T I H D D R R B
C O O K I N G C H I Q O O E
F E R M E N T E D C M T V L
W H I T E I L I V A T S A K
H S D C K S S D C L C E L C
L M H U I T T O E B O D F I
I O D E I M N I I E C A R P
Q T N L R D A T C D O N U U
U H L A I R T S U D N I I C
I E L M H E Y H L A U R T W
D R E C R T Q Q E A T A L W
T N M S D A E L I O B M A N
T Z S V E W C W I N E K S W
```

Solution on Page 319

ART	PAINT
BRAIN	POET
BUILDING	PROCESS
CONCEPTUAL	PRODUCT
CRAFT	SCIENCE
CREATE	SCULPTURE
DANCE	SOLUTION
DESIGN	SPECIAL
DIFFERENT	STORY
DRAW	TALENT
EXPRESSION	TECHNOLOGY
FUN	THEATER
GENIUS	THINKING
GIFT	THOUGHT
IDEA	UNIQUE
IMAGINATION	UNUSUAL
INSIGHT	VISION
INVENTION	WRITER
MUSIC	
NEW	
NOVEL	
ORIGINAL	

```
P O T N E R E F F I D E W Y
A Z Y G O L O N H C E T A R
I X E O R I G I N A L A R O
N T U T Z M S N G I S E D T
T L Q S H A T S I L C R A S
F A I C C G P H E D U C N N
A U N D O I U R E R L M C I
R S U O E N E O O A P I E A
C U S T I A C N H D T X U R
L N I E H T O E C T U E E B
A U U R C I N T P E R C R R
I G I F T O N E A T E A T E
C I S U M N R K V L U F H T
E W L E V O N P I N E A U I
P O E T V I S I O N I N L R
S U I N E G I N S I G H T W
```

ACTION	MARKERS
AIM	MASKS
AMMUNITION	OPPONENT
ARENA	OUTDOORS
ATTACK	PELLETS
BATTLE	PLAYERS
COMBAT	RAMPING
COURSE	RULES
DEFENSE	RUNNING
EXTREME	SPLATTER
FIELD	SPORT
FRIENDS	TARGET
FUN	TEAMS
GAMES	VEST
GEAR	VIOLENT
GOGGLES	WAR
GUNS	WIPING
HIDE	WOODS
HOPPER	
HURT	
KIDS	
LEAGUES	

```
I G E A R E P P O H S D I K
Q N S D N E I R F A R E N A
V I O L E N T H D L E I F L
E P S R O O D T U O Y B R E
S I D E Z E P E A D A U S A
T W S K S A M P F L L V E G
Q Q T R O P S Z O E P J M U
R X U G U N S P S N N S A E
T O Q E W N T H I D E S G S
C E A M M U N I T I O N E T
W F G E A C T I O N I L T E
O M A R K E R S N P G A L L
O A T T A C K U M G B T O L
D N R X R T F A O M T G Y E
S M A E T U R G O A I M Y P
U X W L W S H C B F T W U Z
```

Solution on Page 319

ATHLETIC

BRAND

BUTTON

CASUAL

CLASSIC

CLOTH

COLOR

COMFORT

COTTON

DESIGN

EMBLEM

EMBROIDERED

EXPENSIVE

GOLF

JEANS

KNIT

LACOSTE

LOGO

LOOSE

MEN

PANTS

PLACKET

POCKET

PONY

PREPPY

PROFESSIONAL

RALPH LAUREN

SHIRT

SLACKS

SLEEVE

SPORTS

STYLE

TENNIS

UNIFORM

```
O Z G C M S F H T O L C A W
T U A K O G O L A C O S T E
E N S A J S P O R T S N H K
K I R S I N N E T S T Y L E
C F O E M B R O I D E R E D
O O L J E A N S C C C A T N
P R O F E S S I O N A L I A
R M C L N V S M Y L S P C R
E W T O L S F B S S U H H B
P S E G A O L U L H A L P H
P L K L R E O T A I L A C Y
Y E C T M V O T C R N U Z F
N E A B Y Y S O K T W R F T
O V L E X P E N S I V E I O
P E P C B V D E S I G N T K
M W S T Q C N M T D K E L S
```

Solution on Page 320

BEACHES

CARNIVAL

CONEY ISLAND

COTTON CANDY

DISNEY

EAST COAST

EXPENSIVE

FAMILIES

FERRIS WHEEL

FISHING

FOOD

FUN

GAMES

HOTELS

ICE CREAM

OCEAN CITY

OCEANFRONT

PEDESTRIANS

PEOPLE

PIER

PIZZA

PLANKS

RESTAURANTS

RIDES

RIVERWALK

SANTA CRUZ

SEASIDE

SNACKS

STROLLING

TOURISTS

VIEW

WALKWAY

WATERFRONT

```
O R I V E R W A L K W A Y U
C S T N O R F R E T A W P S
E D S L E T O H E R O O E T
A G N I H S I F H E C E O R
N B E A C H E S W S E D P O
F O O D L N U F S T A I L L
R P E D E S T R I A N S E L
O P I Z Z A I E R U C A X I
N S K C A N S Y R R I E P N
T S A O C T S A E A T S E G
Y L S K N A L P F N Y K N A
E Y D N A C N O T T O C S M
N I C E C R E A M S S C I E
S T S I R U O T R E I P V S
I W E I V Z F A M I L I E S
D L A V I N R A C R I D E S
```

Solution on Page 320

CAB	CITY
CAGE	CLAM
CAKE	CLAP
CALF	CLAW
CALL	CLAY
CALM	CLIP
CAME	CLUB
CAMP	CLUE
CAMS	COAL
CAN	COAT
CAP	CODE
CAR	COIL
CASE	COT
CASH	COW
CAST	CRY
CAT	CUB
CAVE	CUP
CELL	CUT
CHEW	
CHIN	
CHIP	
CHOP	

```
H O T V I T N M C E T N I Y
O Q R U Y A P U S L C F G L
H P A L C T B J L B U D R Q
Z J I C K B R A C F H R X M
W P O H C A U O C C P D F I
M I S I C C T L X V I B E Z
L A F P S G I F C B U L A E
C A L M S P P T Z W Y Y I P
E M A C A M P S Y A V R H M
C G C W C S A A L O P U C T
R L L A C A I C Z T N R I X
Y X G L K A S R W H M F C D
B E G C E E V E K P Y O J T
N L A D P C H E U G A H A G
R T O I A C H I N L F O V P
H C O P A C T C W O C A M B
```

Solution on Page 320

ANCHORAGE

BARROW

BEAR

CANADA

CARIBOU

CLIMATE

COLD

CRUISE

DENALI

ESKIMO

FAIRBANKS

FISHING

FREEZING

FRONTIER

FROZEN

GLACIERS

GOVERNMENT

HUNTING

ICE

IDITAROD

INUIT

JUNEAU

MOOSE

MOUNTAINS

NOME

NORTHERN

OIL

PETROLEUM

PIPELINE

RAIL

ROAD

SALMON

SEWARD

SNOW

TUNDRA

VAST

WEATHER

WILDLIFE

WINTER

YUKON

```
R I D E N A L I J U N E A U
E B S O M O O S E W A R D F
C A N A D A N O K U Y F G R
I R C D F R E E Z I N G N O
G R A S R E I C A L G O I Z
D O R A T I D I T S A V T E
R W I W U T N M F N R E N N
C E B E N N N N U A I G R U O
P F O A D O O E I A N N H M
R I U T R R R L R T I M N E
E L P H A F T O B N H E O E
T D S E I D H R A U S N M S
N L B R L C E T N O I T L I
I I N O N I R E K M F T A U
W W C A Z S N P S W O N S R
L I O M I K S E T A M I L C
```

Solution on Page 320

AMPERE

BARREL

CIRCUIT

COAL

CONDUCTOR

CRUDE OIL

CURRENT

DAM

DIESEL

DIRECT

ENERGY

FILAMENT

FISSION

GROUND

HYDROGEN

INSULATOR

JOULE

KEROSENE

KILOWATT

KINETIC

LANGLEY

LIGHTNING

METHANOL

NUCLEAR

OHM

OPEN

PETROLEUM

POTENTIAL

POWER

PROPANE

REFINERY

RENEWABLE

SHOCK

SWITCH

THERMAL

URANIUM

VOLTAGE

WIND

```
P Y R E N I F E R S H O C K
R O S F I S S I O N L A O C
O G W V Y L A I T N E T O P
P R I E G O T D C V R D A F
A O T S R N T I U C R I C I
N U C L E A R E D M A D A L
E N H R N H O S N R B M I A
P D R K E T T E O P P G E M
O U T E W E A L C E H Y N E
C T T G A M L R R T U E E N
I H A A B T U E N R G L S T
T E W T L D S I A O E G O C
E R O L E B N N R L V N R E
N M L O D G I D U E Q A E R
I A I V Z U Y O H U N L K I
K L K Z M H J O H M W I N D
```

Solution on Page 321

ALBEDO

ANTARCTICA

ATMOSPHERE

BOULDERS

CHANGES

COLDER

CYCLES

EARTH

EXTINCT

FREEZING

FROZEN

GLACIAL AGE

GLACIATIONS

GLACIERS

GREAT LAKES

GREENHOUSE

GREENLAND

HURONIAN

ICE CORES

ICE SHEETS

INTERGLACIALS

LONG

PAST

PLEISTOCENE

POLAR

REDUCTION

SEA LEVEL

SNOW

SUN

TEMPERATURE

TIME PERIOD

WATER

```
W A T E R G N I Z E E R F F
G R E E N H O U S E X T W R
C W E R E H P S O M T A O O
Y R E D U C T I O N I G N Z
C B A C I T C R A T N A S E
L O N P T S A O A O C P G N
E U A G L I E R L E T O L G
S L I L R E M R E D A L A R
T D N A E E I E O P E A C E
E E O C L V A S P C M R I E
E R R I O B E T T E E E A N
H S U A Z T E L L O R C T L
S W H L S U N D A A C I I A
E C H A N G E S O E K E O N
C D P G L A C I E R S E N D
I N T E R G L A C I A L S E
```

Solution on Page 321

ARTICLES	NEW
AUTHOR	OLD
BOOKS	PAGES
BRITANNICA	PEOPLE
CATEGORIES	PRINT
CONTENT	PUBLISH
COUNTRIES	RESEARCH
DICTIONARY	RESOURCE
EDITION	SCIENCE
EDUCATION	SUBJECTS
ENCARTA	TEXT
ENTRIES	TOPICS
EVENTS	WIKIPEDIA
EVERYTHING	WRITTEN
EXPENSIVE	
FACTS	
HISTORY	
KNOWLEDGE	
LANGUAGE	
LEARNING	
LIBRARY	
MEANING	

```
L S E I R T N E T T I R W M
I S T C E J B U S K O O B C
B R E N S E D U C A T I O N
R E X P E N S I V E S U N P
A S T C A V S C I E N C E E
R O I O R R E B I T D F G O
Y U I N C B T R R P L A D P
R R W T H L O I Y G O C E L
O C A E S G E T C T O T L E
T E M N E S H A R L H S W G
S S E T O T L N R O E I O A
I U A E T I N N S N H S N U
H C N N O I T I D E I T K G
H S I L B U P C R W G N U N
C E N C A R T A I P H A G A
E V G W I K I P E D I A P L
```

Solution on Page 321

ADZE

BATTLE AXE

BLADE

BROAD AXE

BRONZE

CAMPING

CHOP

CLIMBING

COPPER

CUT

EDGE

FELL

GRIP

HANDLE

HARVEST

HEAD

HEWING

IRON

LABOR

LEVER

LOG

LUMBER

MEN

SAW

SHAPE

SHOULDER

SIMPLE MACHINE

SPLIT

STEEL

SWING

SYMBOL

THROWING

TIMBER

TOE

TRIM

WEAPON

WIELDING

WOOD

WORK

```
F P S I B W O R K K T V Y L
T R I M X R E D L U O H S O
T I M B E R O B A L E A M F
N O P A E W C A M P I N G Y
F E L L M W W E D A L B N Z
P P E X A E L T T A B Q I Q
T O M S G Q N B S I X I W Q
V U A W N G N I W E H E S B
E L C L I M B I N G V W O E
C P H U W E L D N A H R L P
N Z I M O Z L S E G D E A A
R H N B R N Q D P C V P S H
G E E E H O I X I E H P C S
F A Z R T R R I R N L O G T
U D S Y M B O L G I G C P X
A U W O O D N S T E E L M L
```

Solution on Page 321

ASSEMBLY LINE

CANALS

CAPITALIST

CENTURY

CHANGES

CITIES

COAL

COTTON

CULTURAL

ECONOMY

ELECTRICITY

EMPLOYMENT

ENGINES

GOODS

INDUSTRY

INNOVATION

INVENTION

IRON

JOBS

MACHINES

MANUFACTURING

MILLS

POLLUTION

PROGRESS

RAILROAD

RAILWAYS

STEAM POWER

TECHNOLOGY

TEXTILES

TOOLS

UNIONS

WATERWHEELS

```
C A S B O J C H A N G E S E
I U S L E E H W R E T A W N
T N L S N I N D U S T R Y G
I L V T E C H N O L O G Y I
E Q U E U M A C H I N E S N
S R B U N R B Y M O N O C E
Y C A P I T A L I S T T O S
C O T T O N I L Y R L Y A T
P O L L U T I O N L O L L E
R N O I T A V O N N I N I A
O G N I R U T C A F U N A M
G B Y T I C I R T C E L E P
R A I L W A Y S L A N A C O
E T E X T I L E S D O O G W
S L O O T N E M Y O L P M E
S N O I N U D A O R L I A R
```

Solution on Page 322

LACE	LED
LACK	LEFT
LAD	LEG
LAID	LEND
LAKE	LENS
LAMB	LENT
LAME	LESS
LAMP	LET
LAND	LICK
LANE	LID
LAP	LIE
LAST	LIFE
LATE	LIFT
LAVA	LIP
LAW	LIT
LAY	LOG
LAZY	LOT
LEAD	LOW
LEAF	
LEAK	
LEAN	
LEAP	

```
I R L L O B S R Y T S E Y T
I J J B E L O A S Z C F F X
C L C P M A L E A K C I L H
L M E G F A D Q W A L L O T
A M K M E H L D S E N A L W
S S H H R K C A L A V A L M
Y D R Q K P S A I E N P E Z
B U M A I A C O K D A L A T
M Z P L J E E T N L T F N L
U X B D I L K S L F L E S S
X I V E E T P A E L L E D L
P Y S C K O M L L E N S I V
U G Q N D E A A R G B P T L
N N N S N T Z H W O L R Y Y
L E G Z E Y V O R L H R N Z
X N C H L E T B W R Q K P T
```

Solution on Page 322

BOBS

BREAKERS

COAST

COLLIDE

CRASH

CRESTS

CURL

DISPERSION

DURATION

ENERGY

EROSION

FETCH

FOAM

FREQUENCY

HEIGHT

HIGHS

LOWS

MEDIUM

MOTION

PERIODIC

REFLECTION

REFRACTION

RIPPLE

ROGUE

SEASICK

SPACE

SPLITTING

STORM

SURFACE

SWAY

SWELLS

TIDE

TIME

TRANSVERSE

TROUGHS

TSUNAMIS

UNDERTOW

VIBRATION

WHITECAPS

WIND

```
T S H G U O R T E N E R G Y
N S P L I T T I N G F O A M
H F A B Y B R E A K E R S C
S E H O E C A F R U S Y M I
A T I Y C N N O I T A R U D
R C G G Q O S E M I T U I O
C H H E H I V B U N I N D I
M N S L S T E O O Q D D E R
R O I P P C R I S B E E M E
O I M P A A S S T S E R C P
T T A I C R E W I N D T F M
S A N R E F L E C T I O N O
W R U P T E U G O R L W C T
A B S I I R S W E L L S U I
Y I T E H E R O S I O N R O
D V L O W S E A S I C K L N
```

Solution on Page 322

AERATION	LIGHT
ALGAE	NET
AQUARIUM	OXYGEN
BALANCE	PET
BOWL	PLANT
BUBBLE	POND
CARE	PUMP
CLEAN	RAISING
CORAL	ROCKS
ECOLOGY	SALT
EGGS	SAND
EXOTIC	SHRIMP
FEED	SIZE
FILTER	SWIM
FISH	SYSTEMS
FOOD	TANK
FRESH	VARIETY
GLASS	WATER
GUPPY	
HEATER	
HOBBY	
HOME	

```
D O O F M C G K I E P G V N
T Y X Z P P L I Z S A N D C
B I Y Y O M A I H H A C R W
N B G Y Z I S Q G C L L E K
E J E B Y R S N P L A N T Z
T M N B I H I Y T E I R A V
R Q O O O S K C S A E G E M
O T G H I W I I Q T M K H I
C O R A L T L U L R E T A W
K E R I O L A I F L C M B S
S M G X F R F R B F O A S Q
B H E G I P E B E M L C A V
T S P U S S U E B A O L J V
A I M P H B D M N B G E F J
N F E P K F T C P A Y A P U
K T I Y F B E E E M D N O P
```

Solution on Page 322

AGENCY

AMERICA

BILL

BRANCHES

BUREAU

CABINET

CAPITAL

CIA

COMMERCE

COMMITTEE

CONGRESS

COURT

CURRENCY

DEMOCRAT

EDUCATION

ELECTION

EXECUTIVE

FBI

GRANTS

HOUSE

IMPEACH

IRS

JUDGE

LAW

MILITARY

MONEY

OFFICE

PENTAGON

POLICY

POWER

PRESIDENT

PROCEDURE

REPUBLIC

RULES

SECURITY

SENATE

TAXES

VETO

VOTE

WEALTH

```
R S T N A R G Y E N O M A P
E O S E C U R I T Y Y I M H
W W F S N N O I T C E L E Y
O E B F E I E P N N Z I R C
P A R S I R B E R E N T I I
O L A E R C G A C R O A C L
D T N X S A E N C R I R A O
E H C A E P M I O U T Y J P
M X H T E I E C M C A C N E
O F E E T T I M M O C I O G
C B S C A A O S E C U L G D
R I U N U L L V R O D B A U
A H E R C T L Q C U E U T J
T S T N E D I S E R P P N W
S E L U R A B V E T O E E A
H O U S E R U D E C O R P L
```

Solution on Page 323

ART	NIB
BALL	NOTES
BLACK	OFFICE
BLUE	PEN
BODY	POCKET
BRASS	QUILL
CAP	RED
CHAMBER	ROLL
CHEAP	SCHOOL
COLOR	SIGN
DESK	SMOOTH
DISPOSABLE	STEEL
DOCUMENT	TIP
DRY	TOOL
ERASABLE	WORK
FORMS	WRITE
GEL	
INK	
LEAK	
LID	
MEDIUM	
METAL	

```
H K W K T X S Y X Q K L G S
I X A D I Y R N G E L K A V
Q K S E D D I L C Z L R Q V
B J S R L O U Z S J O O E M
E K C A L B T E T I R W L D
Q U D S K V T P K S F N B F
P U L A L O O H C S O T M V
U P I B N C A P X K R T U S
K R N L K X B A D A M N I B
W H O E L B A S O P S I D P
J U T L O F F I C E L N E P
U T L O O T P B U J E B M Y
R K J U O C H A M B E R E M
I N D I Q M Q L E X T A T G
D W W N G I S L N H S S A C
M I J K T X L D T G C S L X
```

Solution on Page 323

ARCH	FISH
ASH	HATH
BATH	HIGH
BENCH	HUSH
BIRTH	INCH
BLUSH	MATH
BOTH	MOTH
BUNCH	MUCH
BUSH	OATH
CATCH	PATH
CLOTH	PUSH
COACH	RICH
COUGH	RUSH
DEATH	SIGH
DEPTH	SUCH
DISH	WISH
DITCH	WITH
DOUGH	YEAH
DUTCH	
EACH	
EARTH	
FAITH	

```
C H B R A A X D T H K K N E
P N U F H S U B W H T C G R
G D H C R W D A L C B O C J
Y E G I U D E B O U H U M W
I E C N I A A A N S S G S I
I T H A C C T T C O A C H I S
V M T H H H H D E P T H P H
N R U S H F C P U R Z U Q J
E C X T T C T U I T Z H U A
P M I C R L I B M D C P I H
X A H K A O D E W R B H O A
F S T G E T J N A O S S T T
O Z I H G H C C T A F I S H
P H W G K P T H G U O D U L
X Z K I E T N A M N H S U P
C G W S J S O K M K H W T L
```

Solution on Page 323

ASPHALT

BRIDGE

BUS

CAR

CITY

CONNECT

CROSS

DIAMOND

DIVIDED

DRIVE

EAST

ENTER

EXIT

FREEWAY

GRADE

HIGHWAY

LANE

LEFT

LEVELS

LIGHT

LINES

LOOP

MAP

MERGE

PASSING

RAMP

RIGHT

ROAD

ROTARY

ROUTE

SIGN

SPEED

STOP

STREET

TOLL

TRAFFIC

TRAVEL

TRUCKS

TURN

URBAN

```
Y T S F N L H D W W K N H E
A N U R A M P H A M V K L A
N G B R S P E H R O U T E S
L I X Y N A B R U L R N F T
S S L X E M C P G J T R T H
S R S X D I V I D E D A R G
K O I O F G L N R I W C B I
C T A F R E E W A Y Y R S L
U A A X V C R M H T I A E G
R R P E L O O P I D S G N R
T Y L D A N R C G P M I I L
R S S R D N M E H K S G L W
A F P I U E I A W S H O A C
V J E V W C L F A T T T N E
E T E E R T S P Y O O N E R
L W D V Y U I G C P Y O G T
```

Solution on Page 323

BLOSSOMS

BUSINESS

CLASSES

CONSISTS

CROSSES

DISCUSS

DISEASES

DRESSES

FOSSILS

GLASSES

GRASSES

GUESSES

ISSUES

KISSES

LESSONS

LOSSES

MASSES

MESSAGES

MESSES

MISSES

PASSAGES

PASSES

POSSESS

PRESSES

RESTLESS

SADNESS

SAUSAGES

SCISSORS

SEASONS

SEESAWS

SENSES

SESSION

SISTERS

STRESS

SUCCESS

SWISS

SYSTEMS

USELESS

```
S S E C C U S G N L K Q G H
G D R E S S E S O O S M H S
O M G E T W C K I S S E S N
R S U R T S M I S S E S C O
P E E T L S E S S E N D A S
O S S S S E I S E S S A P A
S S S T A E S S S E O C A E
S E E D L E G S G A R R S S
E R S I E E S A O O L M S E
S P S S S T S I S N O C A U
S T A C A U S S D S S X G S
O W M U A R E E S P E P E S
S E N S E S G O S E N M S I
S F O S S I L S E S S A L G
S W I S S B U S I N E S S Z
U S E L E S S Y S T E M S Y
```

Solution on Page 324

AXE

BUILD

CABIN

CEDAR

CHIMNEY

CHINKING

COUNTRY

COZY

DOOR

DWELLING

FOREST

FRONTIER

HEWN

HISTORY

HOME

HOUSE

JOINTS

KNOTS

LAKE

LOG

LUMBER

MORTAR

MUD

OLD

PINE

PIONEER

PRAIRIE

ROOF

ROUND

RURAL

RUSTIC

SHELTER

SIMPLE

TIMBER

TOYS

TREES

WALL

WINDOW

WINTER

WOOD

```
H N K M N S D A A L F J J U
X P U U R O D I T U O L D K
X D N U O R U S T I C U V R
O P R R L R E T N I W B S M
C A L W Y R O T S I H S H U
L C S L O R S T O N K I E E
X E E F A D T G G R Y M L N
R S E T L W N N E Y B P T I
E U R E T I I I U Z I L E P
B O T S B K T L W O E E R C
M H Y A N N H L N C C A X E
I O C I O Z Y E N M I H C D
T Z H R W B E W W R I H L A
L C F L O R T D I N O I A R
H R T F O O R E B M U L K D
C Q Z M D G K A E B M J E W
```

Solution on Page 324

BERRY

BIRD

BLANKET

BLUE JAY

BLUEBELL

BOOK

BUTTERFLY

CAR

CLOTHES

CRAYON

DRESS

EYE

FISH

FLAG

FLOWER

HYDRANGEA

ICE

INK

JEANS

LAKE

MARKER

MOOD

NAVY

OCEAN

PANTS

PEN

POND

POOL

SADNESS

SAPPHIRE

SEA

SHIRT

SKY

SMURF

SOCKS

UNIFORM

VELVET

VIOLETS

WATER

WHALE

```
P E N T P F M Y D V A T D D
Z O Q A N O Y A R C L O O P
Q E N T E K N A L B O O K Z
T T A D B C L I J M D V Q C
S S V G C L O T H E S B F K
I S Y Z M R O F I N U I T O
M E R M V I O L E T S L E W
A N O V E L V E T H A R B F
R D B L U E B E L L I C E R
K A E G N A R D Y H D R A U
E S S H F F W M P R E D O M
R E W O L F H P I T R I H S
A Y K Y A B A B A E N E B O
D E K A G S L W S K C E B C
X T N S L S E S N A E J P K
B P C Q R N P C R X Q I O S
```

Solution on Page 324

ACTION

AUDIENCE

BEAM

BOOTH

BRIGHT

BULB

CAMERA

CINEMA

CORD

DARK

DEVICE

DIGITAL

DOUSER

ELECTRIC

FILM

FLICKER

FORMAT

FRAME

HEAT

HOME

IMAX

LAMP

LARGE

LENS

LIGHT

LOOP

MACHINE

MEDIA

MOVIE

OPTICAL

PICTURE

REEL

SHOW

SHUTTER

SOUND

SPLICE

THREAD

VIEWING

VISUAL

WIDE

```
M W I D E D P O O L E N S N
V I S U A L F T W P M K F N
H A M E N I C O H M O V I E
E M R A D Z H P L G H L K C
A H A R C S R I D L I A I N
T V O E C H F E I B I R U E
I C I M B U I G K D T G B I
V K R A D T H N E C X E U D
D H W C E T N M E G I E L U
N P Y Y R E H L N L M L B A
U D S J U R E I A N A I F E
O B O O T H W C S T X N R M
S P L I C E I U N O I T C A
M A D I I T A M R O F G F R
D A X V P M A L E E R B I F
K J D O U S E R E C I V E D
```

Solution on Page 324

ACADIANS

ACCORDION

ALLIGATOR

ATAKAPA

BOUDIN

CHICKEN

COOKING

CUISINE

DIALECT

ETHNIC GROUP

FAT TUESDAY

FESTIVALS

FIDDLE

FOOD

FRANCE

GUMBO

HOT

ISLAND

JAMBALAYA

LAFAYETTE

LENT

LOUISIANA

MARDI GRAS

NEW ORLEANS

NOVA SCOTIA

OKRA

PEOPLE

QUEBEC

RICE

SAUSAGE

SOUTHERN

SPICY

SWAMPS

VIRGINIA

W F GANONG

100

```
A C O E D I V I M A G E S W
S C O R E N I H C A M N Y A
G N O P V N C O N S O L E U
P L A Y E R O L A T I G I D
P O P U L A R I T Z B W A I
D I S C O M P U T E R N K O
V P Q E P D B S E C I V E D
D I U L E W P F K M A H B N
M E A L R E T C A R A H C E
E D R I A Q I T O N L I N E
T A T K H T I S D N R N M R
S C E S S O H H G C T A S C
Y R R Y N O E I U H G R P S
S A O I O L S I O R E W O P
L J W T D E T P I N B A L L
S O U N D S R A C I N G W P
```

Solution on Page 325

ACID

ANIMAL

ARCHAEOLOGY

ARCTIC

BIODIVERSITY

BLANKET

BROWN

COLD

CONSERVATION

CRANBERRIES

DEAD

DEEP

ENVIRONMENT

FEN

FUEL

GROUND

HABITAT

HARVEST

IRELAND

LICHEN

MARSH

MIRE

MOSS

MUD

PEAT

PLANT

PRECIPITATION

QUAKING

RAIN

SILT

SOIL

SPHAGNUM

SUBSTRATE

SWAMP

VALLEY

VEGETATION

WATER

WET

```
E R I M A R S H N P X Y L B
F Z H U D Q N K O R W G I S
C R A N B E R R I E S O C S
I E R G F E E G T C D L H O
T T V A J T N P A I N O E M
C A E H K A V K V P U E N L
R W S P H R I E R I O A W I
A T T S A T R D E T R H O O
Y B A I B S O N S A G C R S
E L E L I B N A N T L R B B
L A P T T U M L O I A A Z P
L N Y F A S E E C O M C V M
A K U O T N N R S N I I U A
V E G E T A T I O N N D H W
L T N A L P G N I K A U Q S
G A D A E D L O C N I A R G
```

Solution on Page 325

ARTIFICIAL	HOT
BAR	IMPORTED
BEANS	KISSES
BITTER	LIQUOR
BROWN	MELTED
BUTTER	MILK
CACAO	MINT
CAKE	NUTS
CANDY	PIECES
CHIPS	POWDER
COCOA	RAW
COMPOUND	RICH
COOKIES	SOLID
CREAM	SUGAR
DARK	SWEET
DUTCH	SWISS
FAT	VANILLA
FLAKES	WHITE
FUDGE	
GOURMET	
GROUND	
HERSHEY	

```
T B C A S P G V S W E E T T
T W A W C D F Z A G K G J R
H C I R R M R E D W O P E N
A S N A E B C U S U W T U Q
S Y U L A I F O R E T T I B
S F T E M X N M O U S C A Z
S E C E I P E B B K T S H F
D Q X D E T R O P M I O I O
G N L N A B Y E H S R E H K
H I U U R X S E K A L F S R
C O C O A C A C G L I K P A
A E W P R P Y U R L Q N I D
K N U M N G S D K I U Q H U
E V S O L I D L N N O W C K
L A I C I F I T R A R A W W
E T I H W M I N T V C Q K M
```

Solution on Page 325

BEACHES

CATCHES

CHECK

CHEEK

CHEER

CHEESE

CHEST

CHEW

COACHES

COUGHED

EARACHE

HATCHED

HEAD

HEALTH

HEAP

HEAR

HEAT

HEAVEN

HEAVIER

HEAVILY

HEAVY

HEEL

HEIGHT

HELD

HELL

HELMET

HELP

HEM

HENCE

HENS

HER

HIGHEST

HUTCHES

INCHES

KITCHEN

LAUGHED

RICHES

SHE

THE

WHEN

```
M A G T L C H E E R M W K S
H Y V A E H O K P Q X H Y Q
L A Z J W E B U S L E E H L
F X K S T S E E G R E N U H
B O I E W T H A A H S H T E
U G T H X C Y E R C E T C A
J Q C C N R H O A A H D H D
L T H I G H E S T P C E E E
B E E R H T L A E H T H S H
R H N D E H C T A H A C E G
R E E F A E H A E E C A L U
D L V D V L E E S M V A D A
O L A H I M C H E I C S O L
E E E M L E K H E I G H T C
H N H H H Y T Y R H E N C E E
S J E S S A K Z C H E E K W
```

Solution on Page 326

ADAM AND EVE

APPLE JUICE

BLOSSOMS

BRAEBURN

CANDY

CARAMEL

CIDER

COOKING

CRISP

DOCTOR

EAT

FALL

FARMS

FOOD

FORBIDDEN

FRUIT

FUJI

GALA

GRANNY SMITH

GREEN

MCINTOSH

ORCHARDS

PICKING

POLLINATION

RED DELICIOUS

RIPE

ROUND

SAUCE

SEEDS

SKIN

SOUR

STEM

SWEET

TART

TREES

VARIETY

WORM

YELLOW

```
A F C A R A M E L S E E D S
T R E E S L O C P C N P O W
Y T E I R A V R I S O I O E
B X C D M G I U C N I R F E
D N U C D W J R G H T R A T
H R A Q O E C H N F A O C A
L U S L L V L T I O N R S E
Q B L P N E H I K R I S D H
V E P E C D G M C B L A S S
Y A E N C N F S I I L T M M
B R A I I A V Y P D O I O R
G B D K A M D N I D P U S A
X E O S U A U N J E I R S F
R O T C O D Q A U N U F O V
C E Y D N A C R F O F A L L
M R O W M M M G S S R X B C
```

Solution on Page 326

AIRPORT

ASIAN

BRITAIN

BUDDHISM

BUILDING

BUSINESS

CANTONESE

CAPITALIST

CHINESE

CITY

COAST

COMMERCE

CUISINE

CULTURE

DIM SUM

ECONOMY

EDUCATION

FINANCIAL

FOOD

GUANGDONG

HARBOR

INDUSTRY

MANDARIN

POPULATION

REPUBLIC

SHIP

SHOPPING

STAR FERRY

TAOISM

TECHNOLOGY

TERRITORY

TRAVEL

URBAN

```
G E Y R T S U D N I I W B B
N C U I S I N E C N E S R C
I R Y R E P U B L I C I H G
P E R S P O P U L A T I O N
P M R H X N E S P A N Y A I
O M E I Y I S I I E F B C D
H O F P G R T N S R R A G L
S C R L O A T E T U N T U I
Y O A A L D R S R T B E A U
M A T I O N A S O L U R N B
O S S C N A V N P U D R G H
N T A N H M E B R C D I D A
O D S A C S L D I G H T O R
C O I N E D U C A T I O N B
E O A I T A O I S M S R G O
L F N F L D I M S U M Y H R
```

Solution on Page 326

AFRICA

BARBARY

BOAT

BOOKS

CAPTAIN

CARIBBEAN

CREW

CRIMINAL

EYE PATCH

FINES

GOLD

HIGH SEAS

ILLEGAL

KIDNAPPING

LAW

LOOT

MARITIME

MONEY

MURDER

OCEANS

PARROT

PEG LEG

PIRATES

PLUNDER

RAIDS

RANSOM

RIVER

ROBBERY

SABOTAGE

SAIL

SECURITY

SHIPS

SHORE

STEAL

THEFT

TREASURE

VESSELS

VIKINGS

VIOLENCE

WEAPON

```
T G B S L E S S E V G O L D
H N A E M O S N A R A I D S
E I R T H M W E A P O N F A
F P B A S C E C N E L O I V
T P A R K C T W S A C L N S
C A R I B B E A N A L O E H
S N Y P J R E I P E I F S I
T D M Z C S M T G E S L S P
E I A A H I A A R A Y S G S
A K C G R I L U B T R E N K
L S I C N I S O O O E L C I O
Y H R B O A T R V G O U K O
E O F Y E A R I E T O R I B
N R A R G A R P M T T I V L
O E T E P L U N D E R T S A
M U R D E R O B B E R Y V W
```

Solution on Page 326

ANALYSIS

AWAKEN

BEDROOM

BRAIN

COLOR

DARK

DAYDREAM

DEEP

DESIRES

EMOTIONS

EVENTS

FALLING

FANTASY

FEAR

FEELINGS

FLYING

FREUD

JOURNAL

JUNG

LUCID

MEANING

MEMORY

MENTAL

NAKED

NIGHTMARES

ONEIROLOGY

PILLOW

PROPHETIC

REALITY

RECURRING

REM SLEEP

SOUNDS

STORY

STRESS

SURREAL

SYMBOLISM

THE MIND

WAKING

Dream It

```
S O O N E I R O L O G Y D P
U G N I R R U C E R S A E I
R N F G A J D N I A R B M L
R I E H I N U D T K R Q O L
E K A T I L A N R U O J T O
A A R M Y Y A P G P L S I W
L W E A D F R E U D O I O S
I H P R O P H E T I C S N D
T Q E E M S I L O B M Y S N
Y A V S O M O S N P G L X U
M W E T O E S M E D N A S O
E A N R R M F E E L I N G S
N K T E D O D R B C L A R T
T E S S E R I S E D L K S O
A N F S B Y G N I N A E M R
L U C I D G N I Y L F D U Y
```

Solution on Page 327

AFTERLIFE	NIGHT
APPARITION	OCCULT
BEING	PARANORMAL
BELIEF	POLTERGEIST
BOO	RELIGION
CASPER	REVENANT
CASTLE	SCROOGE
DARK	SOUL
DEATH	SPECTRE
DEMONS	SPIRITS
ECTOPLASM	STORIES
FEAR	SUPERNATURAL
FICTION	SUPERSTITION
GHOST TRAINS	WHITE
HALLOWEEN	
HAUNTING	
HORROR	
IMAGE	
KILL	
LITERATURE	
LOCATIONS	
MYTH	

See a Ghost

```
S S B E I N G N I T N U A H
N T E R E L I G I O N P D A
O O L G M S A L P O T C E L
M R I W A S E T I H W P A L
E I E Y W M N T S L E R T O
D E F I C T I O N F U O H W
A S U P E R S T I T I O N E
R E P S A C T L A T L B S E
K T L P U H R N R P A J S N
E N P H G E R G T L U C C O
C A L I T E R A T U R E O Q
A N N F P Y O G S O K I L L
S E A U L A M R O N A R A P
T V S F E A R G H O R R O R
L E P O L T E R G E I S T K
E R T C E P S T I R I P S X
```

Solution on Page 327

PUZZLES • 119

BEAUTY

BLOOMS

BOUQUET

BUDS

BUSH

CLIMBING

COLORS

DOZEN

FLORIST

FLOWERS

FRAGRANT

GENUS ROSA

GIFT

GROW

HIPS

HYBRIDS

LEAVES

LOVE

MINIATURE

NAME

PERFUMES

PETALS

PINK

PLANTS

PRUNING

RED ROSE

ROMANCE

ROSACEAE

SCENT

SHRUB

SMELL

SPECIES

SPRING

SYMBOLISM

TEA

THORNS

VALENTINE

VARIETY

VASE

VINE

```
S E I C E P S D I R B Y H N
G N I N U R P L A N T S G S
U I S N E Z O D E U P N N H
V C M W A L J N A I I R H R
W O O L E O I E H B O Q F U
G L O L C V B H M H G S R B
F O L E A E N I T N E L A V
A R B M S I L O B M Y S G L
B S C S O C H S U B O T R V
O T S I R O L F C R N T A E
P S Y R E D R O S E E R N C
I L E A V E S U C U I E T N
N A M E P D N S Q E S M F A
K T T Q U E R U T A I N I M
V E M B G J O Y V W O R G O
A P E E I B S P R I N G K R
```

Solution on Page 327

VACANT	VIDEO
VACUUM	VIEW
VAGUE	VINE
VAIN	VIOLET
VALLEY	VIOLIN
VALUE	VIRUS
VALVE	VISION
VAN	VISIT
VAPOR	VISUAL
VARIED	VITAL
VARIES	VIVID
VARIETY	VOCAL
VARY	VOICE
VASE	VOLUME
VAST	VOTE
VEIN	VOTING
VERB	VOWEL
VERSE	VOYAGE
VERY	
VESSEL	
VET	
VICTIM	

```
I Z P D V O W E L E S R E V
D E Z D Y E V A S T X H A C
I T N O R K C B O N X G C U
V I I I A O N J R I U R Q J
I L M S V O Y A G E F O K E
V S U V I D E O X V V P D C
E A U N O V V V I T A L A W I
T Z C Y L C E I V A L V E O
O S A A I J R G R E W A I V
V N V D N K Y I N U T L V O
V A R I E T Y V V I S U A L
A I L C O I J L I E T E S U
F W S L J L R N M C S O E M
H L L I E F E A I O T S V E
V W L B O Y K T V A R I E S
H W K P K N F L N A V N M L
```

Solution on Page 327

BANDIT	MATCH
BARS	MONEY
BELLS	MUSIC
BETTING	NEVADA
BONUS	NICKEL
BUTTONS	ODDS
CASH OUT	PAYOUT
CASINOS	PENNY
CHANGE	PLAY
CHERRY	QUARTERS
COINS	REELS
CREDITS	RENO
DOLLAR	SLOTS
FORTUNE	SPINNING
FUN	TILT
GAMBLING	TOKENS
JACKPOT	VIDEO
LAS VEGAS	WINNINGS
LEVER	
LOSING	
LOSSES	
LUCKY	

```
M O N E Y N N E P S B J M S
A Y K C U L A C H E R R Y S
T A T G A P A Y O U T A T W
C I U L A S V E G A S O B Q
H I D Z I M H R E E L S U S
B L F N D T B O L S G A P L
O J O J A Y P L U N R I R L
N S R S X B A B I T N Z B E
U N T I S D L N E N S L U B
S I U G A E N R I T G O T C
N O N V K I S N I D T S T H
E C E C W Y G D O I V I O A
K N I F A C E L L F U N N N
O N Y L C R L E V E R G S G
T O P K C A J C I S U M X E
P O N E R V I D E O D D S J
```

Solution on Page 328

AUTOMOBILES	MARANELLO
AUTOMOTIVE	MASSA
BARCHETTA	MEN
BLACK	MODENA
BRAND	PRANCING HORSE
CARS	RED
CHAMPIONSHIP	RICH
COMPANY	ROAD
COMPETITION	SHELL
CONVERTIBLE	SPEED
DESIGN	STALLION
DRIVER	TESTAROSSA
ENGINE	
ENZO FERRARI	
FACTORY	
FAST	
FIAT GROUP	
FORMULA ONE	
GAS	
GRAN TURISMO	
GRAND PRIX	
ITALIAN	

```
T S A F I A T G R O U P N N
P G E G R A N T U R I S M O
S R F L L E H S E H E A B I
T A A A I D D V S V S A I T
A N C N P B I N I S R D R I
L D T E C R O T A C S E A T
L P O D D I O M H R N S R E
I R R O P M N E O O B I R P
O I Y M O D T G A T C G E M
N X A T E T A L H H U N F O
K H U E A S U D A O R A O C
C A P C O M P A N Y R I Z A
A S S O R A T S E T Q S N R
L L C O N V E R T I B L E S
B X F O L L E N A R A M M Q
E N A I L A T I E N G I N E
```

Solution on Page 328

ACRYLIC

ARTIFICIAL

BAKELITE

BOTTLES

CELLULOSE

CHEMICALS

CLEAR

COLOR

CONTAINERS

CUPS

DURABLE

ENVIRONMENT

FLEXIBLE

HARD

JUG

LANDFILLS

MATERIAL

MELT

MOLDED

NYLON

OIL

PACKAGING

PAPER

PETROLEUM

POLYESTER

POLYMERS

PVC

RECYCLING

STYROFOAM

SYNTHETIC

TABLE

TOXICITY

TOYS

TRASH

TUPPERWARE

WASTE

WRAP

```
W B A K E L I T E L B A T P
R E P A P A C K A G I N G E
A L E N V I R O N M E N T T
P R O L O C I T E H T N Y S
T S R E N I A T N O C V P A
O T E L M F L E X I B L E W
X Y T L A I A C R Y L I C P
I R S A T T L E M R C O D E
C O E N E R A W R E P P U T
I F Y D R A H C L C O S R R
T O L F I S L L D Y L E A O
Y A O I A H U E P C Y L B L
S M P L L L D A T L M T L E
G U J L O L R R O I E T E U
C U P S O N O L Y N R O I M
C H E M I C A L S G S B I N
```

Solution on Page 328

ACTIVITY

AUDUBON

BACKYARD

BINOCULARS

BIRD CALLS

BIRDERS

BIRDING

BOOKS

CAMERA

COMPETITION

EGGS

ENVIRONMENT

FEEDING

FINCH

FLIGHT

FOREST

GROUP

GUIDES

HABITAT

HERON

HOBBY

MIGRATION

NESTING

OBSERVATION

ORNITHOLOGY

OUTDOORS

OWL

PHOTOGRAPHY

RARE

ROBIN

SPECIES

VIDEOGRAPHY

WATCHING

WOODPECKERS

```
E W A T C H I N G U I D E S
G T O V Z H V B I R D E R S
G Y N O I T A V R E S B O R
S H G E D D Y B H E R O N O
B P C O M P E T I T I O N O
S A H S L N E O I T T K I D
N R C C E O O C G V A S B T
O G A K N I H R K R I T O U
I O M L Y I C T I E A T R O
T T E T U A F E I V R P C M
A O R H S C R E P N N S H A
R H A G E M O D E S R E P Y
G P B I R D I N G D T O U B
I S L L A C D R I B I D O B
M A W F R A U D U B O N R O
F O R E S T N E S T I N G H
```

Solution on Page 328

ALUMINUM

ANGLE

ATTIC

BAD LUCK

BUILDING

CARPENTER

CAT LADDER

CLIMB

CONSTRUCTION

EQUIPMENT

EXTENSION

FALL

FIRE

FIXED LADDER

FOLDING

HEIGHT

HOOK

LEAN

LENGTH

PAINT

POOL

PORTABLE

REACH

RIGID

ROOF

ROPE

RUNG

SAFETY

STAIR

STEP

STRINGERS

TALL

TELESCOPING

TOP

TREE

VERTICAL

WALL

WINDOW

WOOD

WORK

```
E R I A T S A W D B M I L C
B E I C P A I N T U R P M B
D A R G D S L W G I L O U V
N C D T I O T L G L K R N E
O H F L F D O R A D E T I R
I J A N U O F W I I X A M T
T E L E S C O P I N G B U I
C R L H O O K R U G G L L C
U E E Q U I P M E N T E A A
R E D D A L D E X I F R R L
T W H P D F E P R O P E M S
S O P T O A E A H E I G H T
N D O U G T L G N I D L O F
O N O I S N E T X E R I F P
C I L A Y T E F A S K R O W
F W G N U R V L L C I T T A
```

Solution on Page 329

ARTICULATE

AXLES

BED

BIG

CONSTRUCTION

DIESEL

DIRT

DRIVER

DUMPING

EMPTY

ENGINE

EQUIPMENT

GRAVEL

HAULING

HYDRAULICS

JOB

LARGE

LIFT

LOADS

MACHINE

MATERIALS

MOTOR

POWER

RENT

SAND

SERVICE

SIDE DUMP

SOD

TIPPING

TIRES

TRAILERS

TRANSFER DUMP

TRANSPORTATION

VEHICLE

WASTE

WEIGHT

WHEELS

WORKERS

```
S D A O L I F T R O T O M D
L P O W E R E N T B O J H H
E G N I P P I T E T S A W N
E N N O I T C U R T S N O C
H I E S U P M U D E D I S A
W P Q O W E I G H T T N A X
P M U D R E F S N A R T N L
U U I I S E R I T L D R D E
S D P E H Y D R A U L I C S
R R M S H E O V I C B D H W
E I E E B P E E N I H C A M
K V N L S H E M P T Y Y U B
R E T N I M A T E R I A L S
O R A C R A L E V A R G I B
W R L F S E R V I C E P N S
T E N I G N E T E L A R G E
```

Solution on Page 329

BAKING

BOILING

BROILING

BUTTER

CHEFS

CUISINE

CULINARY

DESSERTS

DINNER

EATING

EGGS

FISH

FLOUR

FRUITS

FRYING

GOURMET

GRILL

HEAT

HERBS

HOT

LUNCH

MEASURE

MILK

OVEN

PAN

PEPPER

POTATOES

POULTRY

RECIPES

ROASTING

SALT

SAUTEE

SEAFOOD

SIMMER

SKILLET

SPICES

SPOON

STEAMING

SUGAR

UTENSILS

```
D T G J G N I Y R F L O U R
I T L A S T R E S S E D F P
N D O O F A E S P E P P E R
N P D G N I L I O R B O A G
E G N I T A E H T N R G O Z
R R L E E G G S A E U U K N
E U H M V R S P T S R C O T
C T X E I O O T O M U M S S
I E E L R L U A E I E A I P
P N L H F B K T S A U M G I
E S S Z R L S I S T M N Z C
S I O F U T N U E E I I F E
F L Q N I E R E R L N N N S
E S C I T E L L I K S C G G
H H O T S Y P O U L T R Y L
C G N I K A B Z E V S J J C
```

ANCIENT

ART

BLOCKS

BRICK

BUILD

CASTLE

CATHEDRAL

CEMENT

CHISEL

CITIES

CONCRETE

CONSTRUCT

CRAFT

CREATIVE

CUT

FOUNDATION

GEOMETRICAL

GRANITE

GROUT

HAMMER

IGNEOUS

MALLET

MASON

MONUMENT

NATURAL

PYRAMIDS

ROCK

RUBBLE

SAWYERS

SHAPING

SKILL

SLIPFORM

STONE

STRUCTURES

TAJ MAHAL

TOOLS

TRADE

TROWEL

WALL

WORK

```
M O R U B B L E W O R T F M
A T O O L S C E M E N T I A
L T E D A R T L B L O C K S
L A R D E H T A C T A O C O
E J R M N U Y C A S R N I N
T M M U O O R I G A T S R L
S A C R T E I R I C N T B L
H H G O A A A T L U E R G A
D A A T N N N E A M M U I W
T L I P I C S M R D U C G E
N V I T I I R O C K N T N C
E W E U H N F E C C O U E R
I O N C B P G G T S M R O A
C R O F I C I T I E S E U F
N K T L P Y R A M I D S S T
A O S R E Y W A S K I L L C
```

Solution on Page 329

ALLOY

APPLIANCE

AUTOMOBILE

BAR

BEAM

BLADE

BOLTS

BRACE

BRIDGE

BUILDING

CAR

COLD

CONSTRUCT

DURABLE

GRADE

HARD

HEAT

INDUSTRY

KNIFE

MACHINES

MATERIAL

MELT

METAL

MILL

ORE

PLATE

ROD

SHEET

SHIP

SILVER

STAINLESS

STRENGTH

STURDY

SUPERMAN

TEMPER

TOOLS

TOUGH

WELD

WIRE

WOOL

```
I T W I R E V L I S T L O B
T O U G H B D R I T E T P M
L O R E R O S D U R A B L E
E L A I R E T A M E G R A T
M S D Q C S A C M N O A T A
T G S S Y O I S I G T C E L
E K T Q U O N D L T E E L C
M Y U A I P L S L H E W I Y
P E R H E I E L T D H O B C
E P D T U H S R A R S O O L
R R Y B S S S R M J U L M U
J H E E A U G Y L A D C O N
P A R D E R D E F I N K T S
M R M A C H I N E S P R U B
E D Q L E C N A I L P P A O
H C U B M W E L D P V K F R
```

Solution on Page 330

APACHE	MUSIC
BRAVE	NAVAJO
BUFFALO	OKLAHOMA
CASINOS	PILGRIMS
CHEROKEE	PUEBLO
CHEYENNE	RELIGION
CHIEFS	RESPECT
CHIPPEWA	SEMINOLE
CHOCTAW	SEQUOYAH
COMANCHE	SIOUX
CUSTER	TECUMSEH
DAKOTA	TREATIES
ETHNIC	
FEATHERS	
GAMBLING	
GERONIMO	
HOPI	
INDIGENOUS	
IROQUOIS	
JIM THORPE	
LAND	
MOHICANS	

```
R S T O E P I R O Q U O I S
E O E L H H F C I S U M T E
T N C B C J H E T H N I C L
S I U E A I E V A R B N E O
U S M U P M A S Z T G O P N
C A S P A T O K A D H R S I
O C E G C H E R O K E E E M
M W H A M O H A L K O G R E
A I G E W R E L I G I O N S
N O P S Y P W A T C O H C M
C S U O N E G I D N I I H I
H A X P H G N I L B M A G R
E M O H I C A N S I O U X G
U W H A Y O U Q E S D N A L
C H I E F S E I T A E R T I
N A V A J O L A F F U B D P
```

Solution on Page 330

ARENA	MEDALS
AWARD	MONEY
BIT	OWNER
BREED	PONY
BRUSH	PRIZE
CLASS	RACING
COAT	REIN
CONTEST	RIBBON
COURSE	RIDE
CUTTING	RODEO
ENGLISH	SADDLE
EQUINE	SHOW
EVENT	SKILL
FENCE	SPORT
GAIT	TAIL
GROOM	TROT
HARNESS	WALK
HELMET	WINNER
HORSE	
JUDGE	
JUMP	
MANE	

```
S A W N J Z M D T Q U N K U L
L D R A W A E C N E F I E S
L E G E L W D X E S R O H J
O E I Z N K I Y V F P M U J
H R S T H A R N E S S D D W
G B L K E Q U I N E G S H S
U L W Z I C A R G E G L S P
G A I T P L U F L N R A J O
H R S A D D L E I D L D H R
P E I I T U T T S C W E S T
O N R B M I T R H R L M U T
N W L A B U M O O M U C R A
Y O N V C O N T E S T O B X
H E T C N I N T D U O A C K
R N I E R S N W O H S T Q N
G H Y N B Q E G R O O M O C
```

Solution on Page 330

BEAM	OLD
BOAT	PORT
BRIGHT	REEF
BUILDING	ROCK
CAPE	SAFE
CLIFFS	SAILOR
COAST	SAND
DANGER	SEA
DAYMARK	SHIP
FOG	SHORE
GUIDE	SIGNAL
HARBOR	STONE
HAZARDS	TALL
KEEPER	TOWER
LAKE	TRAVEL
LAMP	WARNING
LAND	WATCH
LENS	WAVE
LIGHT	
MAINE	
NIGHT	
OCEAN	

```
Z J C F N S L L A T C W L U
B O R L T D T A O B E A M U
L D L O I U O M I N N T P E
X P N I C F K P Q G K C T E
T E Z A G K F C I A K H S Q
D V D P S H Q S D R A Z A H
P A D I B F T R A V E L O W
C W S H U B S M L R R R C A
C A E S I G Y H O C E A N N
F T B P L A N D O G P W D W
C O V R D K H L N R E S O E
T O G N I N R A W R E A N T
Q L J H N G D K R Y K I B J
G D E R G O H E E B A L U Y
V N C N I G H T E M O O D E
E E F A S X H P F P O R T M
```

Solution on Page 330

ADVICE	PASTA
AIR	PENS
BANANAS	PERFUME
BEANS	PLASTIC
BOLOGNA	POTATOES
BOOKS	RICE
BREAD	SALE
CANDY	SOAP
CHIPS	SOCKS
COFFEE	SODA
COOKIES	SPAGHETTI
COUPON	STICKERS
CRAYONS	TALK
DIRT	TEA
DISCOUNT	TOOTHPICKS
EGGS	TRINKETS
ENVELOPES	USED
GUM	VINYL
JUNK	
MILK	
ONIONS	
PAPER	

```
C I O L G G J D T A L K I U
T S C J D U S O D J J R L R
Q E L Y N I V O N I O N S E
C P I K E M S E O T A T O P
T O O T H P I C K S I M A A
F L O S T S L L O C G S B P
Q E U K G E T A K U T G D C
D V S O I E H E S A N B E H
Z N E O S E R G K T A T E I
W E D B A S S I A N I C D P
W E C O U P O N A P I C E S
P F D I M U G N O V S R L K
E F A Q R O A S D Y F N T C
N O E E L S K A V U A D N O
S C R O T I I I L M D I R T S
H P B E A N S E Y D N A C B
```

Solution on Page 331

ACCENT

AGRICULTURE

ARCH

BREADBASKET

CHICAGO

CITIES

COLUMBUS

CORN BELT

COUNTRY

CROPS

DETROIT

FARMLAND

FLAT

GREAT LAKES

GREAT PLAINS

HEARTLAND

ILLINOIS

INDIANAPOLIS

INDUSTRIAL

IOWA

KANSAS

KENTUCKY

MINNESOTA

MISSOURI

REGION

RELIGIOUS

RURAL

RUST BELT

SMALL TOWNS

ST LOUIS

STATES

WHEAT

WISCONSIN

150

```
T L S P O R C O L U M B U S N
N L L A I R T S U D N I U T
E M A G W C H I C A G O C L
C I R R E G I O N Y I S O O
C N U I B M O N Z G N A R U
A N R C R H W I I I D S N I
N E M U E E A L A F I N B S
I S I L A A E L T A A A E M
S O S T D R P I L R N K L A
N T S U B T C S E M A E T L
O A O R A L I E B L P N I L
C L U E S A T T T A O T O T
S F R F K N I A S N L U R O
I G I R E D E T U D I C T W
W H E A T R S S R U S K E N
H C R A G C O U N T R Y D S
```

ALLEY

ATTIC

BAT

BEARS

BLACK

CAVE

CELLARS

CLOSET

CLOTHES

CLOUDS

COAL

COFFEE

COLOR

CROW

DEATH

ECLIPSE

EVIL

EYES

FOREST

GARAGE

HAIR

HOLE

HORSE

INK

LICORICE

MAGIC

MAHOGANY

MOOD

MOVIE

MYSTERY

NIGHT

PANTHER

SHADOW

SHOES

SKY

SOIL

SPACE

STORM

TAR

TUNNEL

```
M N R Q S R A T U N N E L U
Y E C L I P S E I X R I Q Q
S E A C L O S E T E C H B I
T R G T W F M A H O G A N Y
E N A A T M D T R T T I W E
R B V L R I N I E S O R M L
Y J I O L A C I T E K L N L
L V T I P E G K H R F Y C A
E S E B O H C A O O X F L Q
Y E I V O M T L G F L A O C
E A C R A X O A B V B E U C
S D S A D C S Z E E L M D C
F E C H P X E W O D A H S M
W D L I O S O F L G C R O W
J G N B O T H G I N K O S Q
I K K B Z A S C B O D S I F
```

Solution on Page 331

AIR

BEAD

BIKE

BLACK

BRAKE

CASING

CHANGE

CIRCLE

CYCLE

DUNLOP

FLAT

FRONT

FUN

HOLE

KNOBBY

PARTS

PATCH

PEDAL

POP

PSI

PUMP

RACING

REAR

RIM

ROAD

ROLL

ROTATE

ROUND

RUBBER

SIZE

SLICK

SOLID

SPEED

SPIN

STEM

TIRE

TOUGH

TUBE

VALVE

WHEEL

Bicycle Tire

```
L U M U J B L L O R Q Y L A
L H W Y Q R J M E T S A Y L
M X X E R Y P T R E V L A V
U D Q K R C F U N J H D G Q
Y W K Z Z I R B M G E W H J
T N C C S O T E W P F L A T
L O B R A K E N J O A M C O
R P S D I L O S O S I T Y U
F O L D R E B B U R P O C G
S P I N U G Y U Z K F E L H
F D C B P N N G K K R A E R
O R K I Q A L I N D V L T D
Q S S K R H R O S I N K A V
H B I E O C B T P A C U T A
D T Z L X B L P S I C A O I
A T E M Y X B E A D M N R R
```

Solution on Page 331

ADMIRALS

AIRPLANES

ANNAPOLIS

BASES

BOMBS

BOOT CAMP

BRIG

CHIEF

COMMODORE

COMPASS

CRUISER

DECK HAND

DEFENSE

DESTROYER

DIVERS

ENSIGN

FLEET

FRIGATES

GUNS

LIFEBOATS

MEDALS

MILITARY

NAVY SEALS

NORFOLK

OFFICERS

POLISHED

RADAR

RECRUITING

RESERVES

SAILORS

SHIPS

SUBMARINES

TATTOOS

UNIFORMS

WATER

```
S R O L I A S G I R B C P W
N A P M A C T O O B A O O A
U D N F R I G A T E S M L T
G N I T I U R C E R E M I E
E A A V C O M P A S S O S R
N H B V E O C E L H D D H T
S K O L Y R R A D A R O E A
I C M P U S S S R A N R D T
G E B I D E E T G F L E E T
N D S E N I R A M B U S S O
O E A N N A P O L I S E T O
R F E I H C K B P S Z R R S
F E O F F I C E R S W V O P
O N U S M R O F I N U E Y I
L S X I A D M I R A L S E H
K E Y R A T I L I M N Z R S
```

Solution on Page 332

ACCELERATED

ACTIVE

AGILE

APACE

DASHING

DOUBLE TIME

FAST

FLASHING

FLAT OUT

FLEETING

FULL TILT

HURRIEDLY

HYPERSONIC

IMMEDIATE

IN A FLASH

IN A JIFFY

LIKE A SHOT

LIKE CRAZY

LIKE MAD

NIMBLE

PDQ

POSTHASTE

PROMPTLY

QUICKLY

RAPIDLY

READY

RESPONSIVELY

SNAPPY

SOON

SPEEDY

STRAIGHTAWAY

SUPERSONIC

SWIFTLY

158

```
Y L D E I R R U H R E A D Y
F I S P R O M P T L Y V V Y L
F K U O G N I H S A D L I D I
I E P S N I M B L E T K O I I
J M E T I S H Y T F E U P P
P A A R H H P U A I C B Y D A
A N D S A S E R W R L W P Q R
I E O S A E S A E C A P A G
N V N T L D Z T U O T A L F
A I I E F Y I H S O O N Q L
F T C R T M A G I L E S U E
L C D S E T A I D E M M I E
A A A T O H S A E K I L C T
S F C I N O S R E P Y H K I
H I I F U L L T I L T U L N
E R E S P O N S I V E L Y G
```

Solution on Page 332

BEACH

BULB

CANDLE

CARS

CHILDREN

CLOTHING

COLORS

DAY

DIAMOND

EYES

FIRE

FLASH

GENIUS

GLARE

GLITTER

GLOW

GOLD

HALO

IDEA

JEWELS

LAMP

LIGHT

METAL

MIRRORS

MONITOR

MOON

NEON

RAINBOWS

SHINE

SILVER

SKY

SMART

SMILE

SNOW

SPARK

STAR

SUN

TEETH

WHITE

YELLOW

```
W E T Y T E E T H H Z Y K S
O L E Z E R L C S H I N E E
N A B R V L A A N Y N M Q Y
S W P D I V L M G W H I T E
M W M N T F L O S T O R E C
I F A O D G L D W T P R L H
L G L O W D X I O E A O D I
E I L M Y V E A B D T R N L
B K G A M Q S M N H K S A D
L R D H R G J O I A Z N C R
U A Y C T E D N A L E N E E
B P T A W N G D R O Y T Q N
H S T E E I M O N I T O R A
X S L B M U N U S I L V E R
T S C A R S R O L O C D K U
I O W Y H S Z G N W I U N R
```

Solution on Page 332

ACTORS	PICARD
ADVENTURE	PLANETS
ALIEN	SCIENCE
BEAM	SCOTTY
BONES	SERIES
BOOKS	SHATNER
BRIDGE	SHIP
CAPTAIN	SPACE
DATA	SPOCK
EARTH	STARS
ENTERPRISE	SULU
FANS	TRAVEL
FEDERATION	TREKKIE
FICTION	TRIBBLES
FILM	UHURA
FRANCHISE	VOYAGER
FUTURE	VULCAN
GALAXY	WORMHOLE
KIRK	
KLINGON	
MCCOY	
MOVIE	

```
F R X N O I T A R E D E F W
A V R E N T A H S K O O B E
S S H I P E S I H C N A R F
S E L B B I R T L I D U S S
E I V O M P R U A A T T P U
E R B N R A V T T U E A I L
I E D E E U P A F N C L C U
K S T S L A J G A E E E A V
K N G C C L K L N L B V R O
E L A O O I P L O G R A D Y
R N L T K E E H I K I R K A
T K A T N N M N T N D T M G
B C X Y S R O T C A G A F E
D O Y Y O C C M I E E O A R
V P A W I M L I F B A E N Z
Q S R A T S A R U H U W S R
```

Solution on Page 332

ALPHABET

ARMY

AVIATION

DAHS

DASHES

DECODE

DISTRESS

DITS

DOTS

EMERGENCY

HELP

HISTORY

LANGUAGE

LETTERS

LICENSE

LONG

MARK

MESSAGES

MORSE

NAVIGATION

NUMBERS

NUMERALS

OLD

OPERATOR

PILOTS

PULSES

READ

RECEIVER

RHYTHM

SEQUENCE

SHORT

SIGNALS

SOUNDS

STRAIGHT KEY

TAP

TELEGRAPHIC

TRANSLATE

WAR

WIRE

WPM

```
D R X H I S T O R Y M R A D
W O S D N U O S M P W K R A
D I T S M A R K P U L S E S
W A R S E M E R G E N C Y H
D F A E S L I C E N S E L E
I D N C S T O L I P K N A S
S T S N A V I G A T I O N L
T E L E G R A P H I C I G A
R B A U E S O G A R L T U N
E A T Q S L I T E T E A A G
S H E E D A H V A I T I G I
S P B S R R I P U R T V E S
D L L T D E C O D E E A G H
A A S E C M H T Y H R P N O
E Q H E H U E M O R S E O R
R Q R S A N U M B E R S L T
```

Solution on Page 333

AMERICAN

AUTHOR

BIOGRAPHY

CALIFORNIA

CLASSIC

COOKING SHOW

CULTURE

DINNER

EMMY

FILM

FOOD

FRENCH COOKING

GOURMET

JACQUES PEPIN

JULIE POWELL

KITCHEN

MASTER CHEF

MERYL STREEP

MOVIE

OVEN

PERSONALITY

POTS

PROGRAMS

PUBLIC

RECIPES

SMITH COLLEGE

SMITHSONIAN

SPY

TALL

TV SHOW

VOICE

WAY TO COOK

WINE

WOMEN

```
Q A P P M K O O C O T Y A W
W I N E A R E C I P E S F O
F N I R S O C S E U I J I H
N R P S T H I P R B V U L S
Y O E O E T S Y U L O L M G
H F P N R U S N T I M I P N
P I S A C A A A L C T E R I
A L E L H H L I U H E P O K
R A U I E L C N C R A O G O
G C Q T F B E O T W M W R O
O D C Y S H L S O N E E A C
I O A N C L L H K K R L M E
B O J T E Y S T O P I L S M
W F I G R V O I C E C N M M
G K E E T W O M E N A G G Y
T E M R U O G S R E N N I D
```

Solution on Page 333

ACADEMY AWARD

ANIMATION

BEAST

CAMERON DIAZ

CHARACTERS

CHILDREN

COMEDY

DISNEY

DONKEY

DREAMWORKS

DVD

EDDIE MURPHY

FAIRY TALES

FAMILY

FANTASY

FILM

JOHN LITHGOW

KIDS

KING

KISS

KNIGHT

LORD FARQUAAD

LOVE

MIKE MYERS

MONSTER

MOVIES

MUSICAL

OGRE

PIXAR

PRINCESS FIONA

PUSS IN BOOTS

RESCUE

SHREK

VIDEO GAMES

```
D V D R E A M W O R K S K T
L O G R E T S N O M I Z E S
P U S S I N B O O T S M R A
S R E T C A R A H C S I H E
L V I D E O G A M E S K S B
J O H N L I T H G O W E Z A
P N R X C S E I V O M M A N
I E D D I E M U R P H Y I I
K I N G F L S L C P Y E D M
Y S A T N A F S I S D R N A
K N I G H T R X F F E S O T
D O N K E Y A Q L I M R R I
C H I L D R E N U L O V E O
Q D L A C I S U M A C N M N
S D R A W A Y M E D A C A O
Y L I M A F Y E N S I D C K
```

Solution on Page 333

ANIMAL	PEOPLE
AXLE	PLOUGH
BIT	PULL
BUCKBOARD	RIDE
BUGGY	ROAD
CAB	ROMANTIC
CHARIOT	SCHOONER
COACH	SEAT
COUNTRY	SLED
DRAY	STREET
DRIVE	SULKY
EQUIPMENT	SURREY
FARM	TEAM
GIG	TRAP
HARNESS	VEHICLE
HORSE	WAGON
LOAD	WHEEL
MULE	WHIP
OLD	
OXEN	
PARK	
PASSENGER	

```
U X G G K R A P L O U G H W
G F S B L Y D W A G O N D B
F Y T E E R T S M A E T A L
Q A D R A E L C I H E V L F
Z I R Y O T X H N J Y L L L
R U E M W M B O A R H I U F
S Q L H D N A O T D O D P M
C I P A S S E N G E R F Z C
D A O R R T U E T A S I O F
L L E N S O I R O I E A V L
O L P E C Y S B G L C P I E
P M H S U L K Y X H Q A Y E
T U K S G C H A R I O T B H
U R E Q U I P M E N T X L W
H E A B U G G Y A X S L E D
S Q L P I H W R X S B R T N
```

Solution on Page 333

ALGERIA

ARID

ASIA

BERBERS

BIG

CAMELS

CHAD

CHEETAH

DESERT

DROUGHT

DUST

ECOREGIONS

EGYPTIANS

FLAT

GAZELLE

GOATS

HEAT

HOT

LANDFORM

LARGE

LIBYA

LIZARDS

MASSIVE

MOROCCO

MOUNTAINS

NIGER

NOMADS

PLAINS

PLATEAUS

RED SEA

SAHARA

SCORPION

SUDAN

TIMBUKTU

TRADE

TUNISIA

VIPER

WATER

WIND

WOODLANDS

```
S U D A N I G E R E D S E A
N E M R E T A W I N D P L R
Q D L O X A I R E G L A L A
D A I S U H N O M A D S E H
U R Z N D N B H T E J S Z A
S T A O G N T E L E N I A S
T O R I W J A A R A G V G T
A C D G T U N L I B A R R M
L C S E S D D T D N E E A A
F O C R F A P I N O S R I L
C R O O H Y H M R E O S S I
A O R C G I B B B D A A W I B
M M P E D R O U G H T O N Y
E V I S S A M K O T A U U A
L S O C H E E T A H E A T U
S S N I A L P U V I P E R P
```

Solution on Page 334

ANGUS

ANIMAL

BOVINES

BRISKET

BROILING

BULL

CALF

CATTLE

CHICKEN

CHUCK

COOKING

COWS

CUISINE

CUTS

DINNER

FARM

FEED

FILET

FLANK

FOOD

GRILL

HAMBURGER

INDUSTRY

JERKY

KOBE

LEAN

MEATLOAF

POT ROAST

PRIME RIB

PROCESSED

PROTEIN

RANCHER

RARE

RECIPES

RED MEAT

SANDWICH

SHANK

SIRLOIN

SMOKED

STEAKS

```
G C U I S I N E J F C R I C
N F F A A B C H I C K E N O
L A M I N A R L Z B O C D W
E R E N D G E O B U B I U S
L M L L W T U G I L E P S T
T E K S I R B S R L K E T E
T P R O C E S S E D I S R A
A F V H H T Y V M R A N Y K
C F U S H A N K I O A P G S
T C G H A M B U R G E R N I
K A R D E E F T P E I O I R
N M E A T L O A F L J T K L
A C N M A P P K L J P E O O
L U N C D E K O M S J I O I
F T I K S E N I V O B N C N
P S D O O F R E H C N A R B
```

Solution on Page 334

ARSON

ASH

BURNING

CANDLE

CHARCOAL

COLOR

COMBUSTION

CONTROLLED

COOKING

DAMAGE

DANGER

DRILL

EMBER

EXTINGUISH

FLAMMABLE

FUEL

GLOW

HEAT

HOUSE

HUMAN

ICE

IGNITE

KINDLING

LIGHT

MEN

OIL

ORANGE

OXYGEN

PROCESS

RED

SMOKE

SOOT

STATION

STOVE

TINDER

WARM

WATER

WILD

WOOD

YELLOW

```
A W N D I W W C S C E J W W
B T L R O O O O A E S F D A A
T D E L L O R T N O C U T R
I M G L K S H E O O D Z E M
N Q E I O G G L M T A B R L
D Y N N I Y A B C R M J W Q
E G N L X O U A I E A I D A
R X P O C S N M G G G H W G
P N T R T D W M N N E O U Y
R R A I L P I A I A O B E K
O H O E N V L L T D U L V I
C N M J U G D F E R O L O C
E S U O H N U O N D I I T E
S T A T I O N I H D E R S O
S M O K E L N H S A S D N F
T O R A N G E C Z H U M A N
```

Solution on Page 334

BAG

BLADE

CATCHER

CHORES

CLIPPINGS

CUT

CYLINDER

ENGINE

FIELD

GAS

GRASS

HANDLE

HOME

LANDSCAPE

LAWN

MACHINE

MANUAL

MOW

MULCH

OIL

POWER

PUSH

RACING

REEL

RESIDENTIAL

RIDE

ROBOTIC

ROTARY

ROUNDS

SAFETY

SUMMER

TOOL

TORO

TRIM

WEEDS

WHEEL

YARD

```
I M N L D G N E N N R S S F
R M W R O G R P S R D E R E
T L A U N A M A E N E P E L
E Y L C S B F D U H P D W L
C I R V H E N O F C A W O M
A T T C T I R O I L C I P L
T U M Y L O N O B U S I G S
C E O Y Z I R E H M D W C M
H S C E D G P O N C N H N H
E R A N N R Z P I T A E D G
R E S I D E N T I A L E L R
M U C G T W O H A N D L E A
I A W N E B T R O Q G M I S
R I D E O O K G G M M S F S
T P D R O T A R Y U E S G Y
H S F L U S P U S H G V D Q
```

Solution on Page 334

AMERICA	ROUTES
CARS	SCHEDULES
CHICAGO	SEATS
CITIES	SERVICE
COACH	SLEEPER
COMMUTER	SLOW
COMPANY	SPEED
DIESEL	STATIONS
DINING	TICKETS
ENGINE	TRACKS
FARE	TRAINS
FAST	TRAVEL
FEDERAL	TRIP
FUNDS	TUNNELS
GOVERNMENT	USA
INTERCITY	VANCOUVER
LOCOMOTIVE	VIEW
NATIONAL	WASHINGTON
NIXON	
PUBLIC	
RAILROAD	
RAILWAY	

```
T R A I N S P E E D F A R E
N O X L A R E D E F L E S C
O U S K C A R T R A Y N C I
X T L S I C V E N T O G O V
I E O L R I T O I I R I A R
N S C O E U I C T E I N C E
Y T O W M T R A P L C E H S
L E M M A E T E A O S S I A
E K O N T S E L U D E H C S
V C T N A L H V G A I U A L
A I I F S Q E I T N T S G E
R T V P I R T S N K I A O S
T N E M N R E V O G C N V E
F U N D S L E N N U T H I I
Y A W L I A R A I L R O A D
L T P U B L I C O M P A N Y
```

Solution on Page 335

ACTOR

AMERICAN

ART

AUDIENCE

BALLET

BROADWAY

BURLESQUE

CAST

COMEDY

COSTUMES

CULTURE

CURTAIN

DANCE

DIALOGUE

DIRECTOR

DRAMA

EVENTS

FILMS

LIGHTS

MOVIE

MUSIC

NATIONAL

NEW YORK

OPERA

PLAY

PROPS

REALISM

REGIONAL

RENT

REVIVAL

SCENERY

SEATS

SHOW

SINGING

SONDHEIM

STAGE

STORY

TICKET

TRAGEDY

WESTERN

Theater of the United States

```
N T E K C I T S A C W O H S
K R O Y W E N D R A M A T P
S A E E C U R T A I N Z H R
E G A T S Q S S T N E V E O
P E C L S S M L I F C G U P
J D L A M E R I C A N E G S
N Y L N O L W G Y D E M O C
G R A O V R E F I C I N L A
N O N I I U B R O A D W A Y
I T O T E B E S U H U L I R
G S I A T C T S E T A F D E
N T G N T U T I E V L I V N
I U E O M H M L I J P U P E
S R R E G U L V M U S I C C
F M S I L A E R N S T A E S
Y A L P B R O T C A R E P O
```

Solution on Page 335

PUZZLES • 183

ACID ROCK

ALBUMS

AMPLIFIER

BAND

BARITONE

BLUES

CONCERTS

DEATH

DRUGS

ENGLAND

FAMOUS

FEEDBACK

FIRE

FOXY LADY

FREEDOM

GUITARIST

HARD ROCK

HEROIN

HEY JOE

HIPPIE

LEGACY

LONDON

LSD

MARIJUANA

MONTEREY

MOVIE

MUSICIAN

OVERDOSE

POPULAR

PRODUCER

RECORDING

SCARVES

SEATTLE

SINGER

SIXTIES

VIETNAM

WOODSTOCK

```
E R I F R S U O M A F N N E
K C A B D E E F R D H A O N
W C E A B A I G A O T I D G
D O S N L T H F C S A C N L
R N O D U T M F I Y E I O A
U C D D E L R R D L D S L N
G E R L S E A A R R P U C D
S R E S E T L M O E O M H M
I T V D I Y O C C G P A A A
X S O U X N E C K N U R R N
T M G O T R R C K I L I D T
I F F E I P P I H S A J R E
E S R E C U D O R P R U O I
S E V R A C S M U B L A C V
Y C A G E L H E R O I N K O
H E Y J O E N O T I R A B M
```

Solution on Page 335

ANIMALS

CAMOUFLAGE

CHORDATA

CUTE

DOLICHOHIPPUS

DOMESTICATED

ENDANGERED

EQUINE

EQUUS ZEBRA

FOREST

FUR

GALLOP

GRASSLANDS

GRAZER

HABITAT

HAREMS

HERDS

HIPPOTIGRIS

HOOF

HORSES

MAMMALS

MANES

PATTERN

PLAINS ZEBRA

PREDATOR

QUAGGA

RARE

SAVANNAS

SPECIES

STALLION

TAIL

UNGULATE

WILD

WOODLANDS

ZEBROID

ZOO

AFRICAN
ARTISTS
BEATS
BEENIE MAN
BLUES
BOB MARLEY
DANCEHALL
DUB
FESTIVAL
HORNS
ISLAND RECORDS
JAMAICAN
KEYBOARDS
LOVE
LYRICS
MUSIC GENRE
MUSICIANS
ORGAN
PEACE
PERCUSSION
PETER TOSH
POLITICAL

RASTAFARI
RHYTHM
ROCKSTEADY
SINGER
SKANK
SNARE DRUM
STYLE
SWING TIME
TEMPO
THE WAILERS
WALKING BASS

Zebras Are Cool

```
T A I L Z E B R O I D L I W
Y U N G U L A T E Q U I N E
D W O O D L A N D S E N A M
S O I N E G A L F U O M A C
P G L A T A D R O H C U T E
E R L I A R B E Z S U U Q E
C A A T C S L A M I N A N N
I S T A I H A G G A U Q R D
E S S T T R O N A Z O O E A
S L E I S E H H N L T X T N
M A R B E Z S N I A L P T G
E N O A M A T M D P V O A E
R D F H O R S E S Y P A P R
A S O K D G R A R E Q U S E
H O H I P P O T I G R I S D
F U R M A M M A L S D R E H
```

Solution on Page 335

ANGER

BABY

BAWL

CHILD

CRY

DUCT

EMOTION

EYES

FEELING

GRIEF

HAPPY

HORMONES

HUMANS

HURT

INFANT

JOY

LAUGHING

LOSS

LOUD

MOANING

NEWBORN

NONVERBAL

ONIONS

PAIN

REFLEXIVE

RELEASE

RESPONSE

SAD

SHEDDING

SOB

STRESS

TANTRUM

TEAR

TISSUES

TODDLER

UPSET

WAIL

WEDDING

WEEP

WHINING

```
G N W H I N I N G C H   J O Y
P N O I T O M E E U J R B C
R T I S S U E S R W P A S F
H W R D R A E T F C B S S F
Q N E S D R S N O I N O E C
U V O E Z E S N O P S E R T
A E W N P F H C H I L D T N
N T E O V L A S N I A P S S
G A D M S E Y G N I N A O M
E N D R E X R G G D W B L K
R T I O Y I C B A W L O U D
H R N H E V E S A E L E R G
A U G F G E M R E L D D O T
P M K A H U M A N S S O L C
P M G I N F A N T I D T G U
Y O A A A W A I L Y W P G B D
```

Solution on Page 336

```
J X I J S E M I T G N I W S
T L B R A R S B E A T S I N E
E L A O A M E T S T Y L E A
M A W V B F A L S T R A C G
P H F A I M A I I I F N A R
O E T R L T A T C A T D E O
L C T Y I K S R S A W R P C
I N N E H C I E L A N E A K
T A F A R R A N F E R C H S
I D U B M T Q N G C Y O B T
C I S E U E O C U B T R L E
A S N A I C I S U M A D U A
L Y R I C S S N H L D S E D
E V O L U I P R E G N I S Y
Y X H M O M U R D E R A N S
S K A N K S D R A O B Y E K
```

AUTO	PLANT
AVALON	POPULAR
BRAND	PRIUS
CAR	QUALITY
COMPACT	ROBOTS
COROLLA	SAFETY
DEALERS	SALES
DESIGN	SCION
DRIVE	SEDAN
ENGINE	SIENNA
FACTORY	SUV
FOREIGN	TACOMA
GLOBAL	TERCEL
HYBRID	TMC
IMPORT	TOKYO
JAPAN	TRUCK
LEXUS	TUNDRA
LOGO	YARIS
MATRIX	
MODELS	
MOTOR	
PARTS	

```
W A Q M R J W T Q J S M S B
O M S I S G W O Y O A A P T
Y S A F E T Y S T M L P L V
K P F T H M S U X E L T A K
O G O L R Y A V S E A N N N
T R O P M I B O C C N Q T O
M P R I U S X R O E Y U R I
D N A R B L E M I C R A U C
T L M T O T A S O D O L C S
U A O W M B F R W E T I K I
N B D B F C O M P A C T E R
D O E E A L R T E L A Y N A
R L L R L O E V S E F R I Y
A G S A T X I S T R A P G R
N E F O V R G D E S I G N S
G W M M D A N C W N A D E S
```

Solution on Page 336

ANXIOUS	JEALOUS
AUGUST	JUST
BLUSH	MINUS
BUS	MUSCLE
CACTUS	MUSIC
CHORUS	MUST
CIRCUS	PLUS
CLUSTER	PUSH
COUSIN	RADIUS
CURIOUS	RUSH
CUSHION	RUST
CUSTOM	STATUS
DISCUSS	THUS
DUSK	TUSKS
DUST	USE
EXHAUST	USING
FAMOUS	USUAL
FOCUS	VIRUS
FURIOUS	
GENIUS	
HUSBAND	
HUSH	

```
E O R N E K T E F Z K O O N
R B U B N F J S L Q F E J S
S G S T A T U S U C R I C U
L N H C A C T U S M S C D O
G I S J E A L O U S H U V M
J S U I D A R I O O S I M A
J U L V U N K R R T R T M F
T U B G S X A U G U S T U X
H U S H K I S C S U P R U G
S L S T K O L V A D I D E L
U M K K C U S H I O N N A F
P T O I S S X S U A I U O A
A S S T U E C S B U S C S M
S U E N S U O S S U U U Z E
M R I U S U U Y L S O V H G
M M B S W H C P L B C X H T
```

Solution on Page 336

AIR RACING

AIRPLANE

AMERICAN

ATCHISON

AUTHOR

AVIATION

AVIATRIX

BIPLANE

BRAVE

CELEBRITY

COURAGE

CRASH

DES MOINES

EUROPE

EXPERIENCE

FASHION

FEMALE

FEMINIST

FIRST

HERO

HISTORICAL

ICON

KANSAS

KNOWLEDGE

LEGEND

LOST

MARY

MISSING

MYSTERY

NURSING

PILOT

PIONEER

RECORDS

SCIENCE

SEARCH

SKILL

USA

WAR

WIFE

WOMAN

Solution on Page

```
G W Y R E T S Y M A R Y O X
C N O S I H C T A W I F E F
R O I M U S A I R P L A N E
S N U S A M E R I C A N A M
E F O R R N E B O R E H L I
A A G I A U C E I C O N P N
R S N A T G N L N W B A I I
C H I U G A E E H R A I B S
H I S T O R I C A L J R Q T
M O S H D C R V E P O R U E
H N I O S E E S A S N A K C
T T M R E L P S D R O C E R
O S C N A A X I R T A I V A
L R O M Y D E S M O I N E S
I I E L K N O W L E D G E H
P F D N E G E L L I K S Y U
```

Solution on Page 337

AIR

BALL

BUCKET

CAVITY

CHAMBER

CLEAN

DEVICE

DIAPHRAGM

DRINKING

FLOW

FLUID

FUEL

HOSE

HYDRAULIC

INFLATE

LABOR

LEISURE

LEVER

LIFT

LIQUID

MANUAL

MARINE

MOVE

OPERATOR

PISTON

PLUNGER

PRESSURE

PUMP

ROTARY

RURAL

SIPHON

SUCTION

TANK

TIRE

TOOL

VALVE

VILLAGE

WATER

WELL

WORK

```
V W U T R S P U M P P T X A
N A A G R Z C T O O L I I J
A O L T M A N U A L V R S P
E N H V E G D E V I C E U P
L F O P E R A T O R Y T C L
C R H T I S O R E O R A T U
T V T F S S O B H Z O L I N
A P E I F I M H E P B F O G
N A R L U A P C G F A N N E
K O U E H Y D R A U L I C R
F I S C S W J E L V K O D O
D T I L E S N R L N I L W T
L R E L D I U Q I L E T Y A
N U L I R R B R V V G I Y R
F A G A A C D T E K C U B Y
B K M L Y K K R O W W X O N
```

Solution on Page 337

AIRPLANE	LION
ANIMAL	LIZARD
BACK	LONG
BALANCE	MAMMALS
BIRD	MONKEY
BODY	MOUSE
BOTTOM	PART
CAT	PIG
CHASE	PONY
COW	RAT
CURLY	REAR
DEER	REPTILES
DOG	RUMP
END	SCUT
FEATHERS	SECTION
FISH	SWISH
FLEXIBLE	TORSO
FOX	WAG
FURRY	
HAIR	
HORSE	
KITE	

200

```
N A D K T T Q T R S U S O U L
L H Y D U A E S A H C U W V
N J M K R M O N K E Y U W F
A Z F E Y A I X M E X U T T
F O T E C M Z Y R D P O N Y
X I Y V A N O I T C E S Y E
K V S L M T A F L B I R D L
B W E H A H H L Q W E O O R
C B L O M A D E A A O T B G
O X I T M C N X R B A C K I
G K T R A A E I M S L M V P
H C P A L T A B O T T O M W
S O E P S I Y L R U C U N A
Y R R U F K O E A E R S A G
P I H S I W S N T B E E P O
A S A D E A F E T G W D Y D
```

Solution on Page 337

ARBOR	OLD
BARK	PLANT
BED	QUERCUS
BRANCH	RED
CABINET	ROOT
CATKINS	SEED
CHAIR	SHADE
CHEST	SHRUB
CORK	STRONG
DESK	STURDY
DOORS	TABLE
DURABLE	TALL
FLOWERS	TANNIN
FRUIT	TRUNK
GROW	WATER
HABITAT	WHITE
HARD	WINE
LARGE	WOOD
LEAF	
LIVE	
MIGHTY	
NUT	

Oak

```
M H A S A K S E D G B K K L
S H A D E J B E T T N C T L
I Y O O W E O Q O I H W E A
I O D O G L D O N A H A J T
W S R R D B R N I K F W J I
P G A S U A A R B O R H I E
R L C P Y T H G I M U A K E
V I A V Y R S C H E I F B W
T V R N E U T D N C T E D P
S E O T T N W E A A T U N E
D H A G X K R B B U R H S C
P W D N S N I K T A C B E B
Q I D O K N H A B I T A T B
F N M R E T F L O W E R S N
H E O T Q U E R C U S C T H
R C T S E H C F J P O J A B
```

Solution on Page 337

PUZZLES • **203**

ACADIA

AMERICA

BANGOR

BAR HARBOR

BEACHES

BLUEBERRY

BOAT

CANADA

CHICKADEE

CLAMS

COASTLINE

COLD

CRAB

EAST COAST

FISHING

FORESTS

HUNTING

ISLAND

LOBSTERS

MAINE COON

MAPLE SYRUP

MOUNTAINS

NEW ENGLAND

NORTH ROCK

NORTHERN

PINE TREE

PORTLAND

SALMON

SCENERY

SEAFOOD

SHIPBUILDING

SNOW

USA

WINTER

WOODS

```
R U A I P A D K C A N A D A
O W M S U I W C N E H S O L
G I E L R D O O T A N U O O
N N R A Y A O R A S O Y F B
A T I N S C D H O T R R A S
B E C D E A S T B C T R E T
P R A N L W R R M O H E S E
N I I R P I E O D A E B C R
O A N H A S U N R S R E H S
M B F E M N A B G T N U I T
L A E A T L O N P L E L C S
A R L A T R I G S I A B K E
S C I R C T E U F N H N A R
Q N O O N H W E Q E O S D O
S P L U Y R E N E C S W E F
V D H G N I H S I F A Q E X
```

Solution on Page 338

BAIT

BOAT

CAST

CATCH

COMMERCIAL

CORACLE

CRAB

DIP

DRIFT

FISH

FLOAT

HAND

HAUL

HOLD

HOOK

KNOT

LAKE

LURE

MESH

NET

NYLON

OCEAN

PLANKTON

POLE

RIVER

ROD

SALMON

SCOOP

SEA

SHRIMP

SILK

SNAGGING

TACKLE

TANGLE

THREAD

TRAP

WATER

WOOL

WORK

```
C L E B E H A K G J C H H S
K T B O G A X T H C M W M Z
K R P L A N K T O N Y Q B P
L A C O Y D I M A H K O O H
W P N L C D M G F C A S R I
X E O T U E V O G T A O L F
W N L O R A A F S A L M O N
T S P C C E H N I C N Z D O
T E I I A S T Z P S W S B W
B A E L D R D A E R H T A O
L E C R K L O B W R E V I R
P R I K O I C C I B R A T K
L F W H L E X M A H E R N Y
T A N G L E P R T S L O O W
E J K O A H C H E E T D S I
W Q P E R U L I U M N I P D
```

Solution on Page 338

ATTACH	FATTY
ATTACK	FITTED
ATTEMPT	HOTTER
ATTEND	KETTLE
ATTIC	KITTEN
ATTRACT	LATTER
BATTER	LETTER
BATTING	LITTER
BATTLE	LITTLE
BETTER	MATTER
BETTING	NETTED
BITTEN	PATTED
BITTER	POTTED
BOTTLE	PRETTY
BOTTOM	RATTLE
BUTTON	SETTEE
CATTLE	SETTLE
CHATTER	UTTER
COTTAGE	
COTTON	
DOTTED	
FATTER	

```
R R E T T A H C O F E D D D
N E T P M E T T A R L E E R
E T T G N I T T A B T T E E
T T R T C R T T R T T T L T
T A E I E Y T E O A A I T T
E L T T I L T D P M C F T A
D T T P E T J G N I T T E B
A I A G E D D A R Y C G K S
L B M B M H N A T T A C H E
K D M Z O B N E T T I B H L
I E O O U T L O T U A O L T
T T T T Q T T T O T T T C V T
T T T Y T K C L E T A T K E
E O O A F A T T E R O E E S
N P B I T T E R U A M C Z R
Q Y T T E R P E E T T E S X
```

Solution on Page 338

ACTIVIST

ALABAMA

ATLANTA

BAPTIST

BLACK

CHILDREN

CHURCH

CORETTA

COURAGE

EQUALITY

FATHER

FREEDOM

GEORGIA

HISTORY

HOPE

ICON

JAIL

KILLED

LEADER

LEGACY

MARCHES

MEMPHIS

MINISTER

MOVEMENT

NAACP

ORATOR

PEACEFUL

PREACHER

PROTEST

RACISM

RELIGION

REVEREND

SELMA

SHOT

SOUTH

SPEAKER

SPEECH

STRUGGLE

```
H G E O R G I A T N A L T A
I Q R Y C A G E L M O S V S
S D N E R E V E R A S P S O
T H A L L A V A O R B E E U
O C A G S I T P T C C A L T
R R C G P T G M A H O K M H
Y U P U E T T I R E U E A A
T H K R E O S N O S R R E L
I C O T C H M I E N A N U P
L C H S H S C S T M G F R S
A C T I V I S T I P E E H I
U D E L L I K E K C A V H H
Q O L E A D E R A C A B O P
E F A T H E R E H B A R P M
T S E T O R P E J A I L E E
I M O D E E R F N O C I B M
```

Solution on Page 338

BAKED POTATO

BOILED

BUTTER

CARBOHYDRATES

CHIVES

COOK

CROP

CULTIVATED

DINNER

EYES

FAMINE

FLAKES

FOOD

GARDEN

GRAVY

GROUND

HASH BROWNS

MEAT

NUTRITION

PANCAKES

PEEL

PLANT

POTASSIUM

RED

ROOT

RUSSET

SALAD

SCALLOPED

SKINS

SOLANACEAE

SPUDS

STAPLE

STARCHY

SWEET

TOPPINGS

TUBER

VEGETABLES

WHITE

YAM

YUKON GOLD

```
E F P E E L R Y B F N M J Y
C G S L P J E U H U U E V C
U A D Y A M B K C C T A E O
L R R E D N U O R G R T T O
T D S B P T T N O G I A E K
I E B E O O C G P H T N T R
V N S O K H L O W O I S S S
A S R S I A Y L P M O E N E
T S N V U L L D A N N L W Y
E Y E I K R E F R C X B O E
D S Q K K K M D X A S A R D
F P O T A S S I U M T T B I
O G B B N C S T A P L E H N
O T O P P I N G S A B G S N
D A L A S O L A N A C E A E
R T E E W S D U P S Y V H R
```

Solution on Page 339

ACOUSTIC

AIR

ALARM

AMPLITUDE

BARRIER

BOOM

BUZZ

CLAP

CRASH

DECIBEL

DIN

EAR

ECHO

ENERGY

FREQUENCY

LEVEL

LISTEN

LOW

MUSIC

NOISE

PHYSICS

PIANO

PITCH

PRESSURE

RING

SENSE

SILENCE

SINGING

SOFT

SONG

STATIC

STEREO

TALKING

THUNDER

TONE

TRANSMIT

VOICE

VOLUME

WAVE

YELLING

Sound

```
S O I V M F N M E P I T C H
J I W O P I A N O E R E T S
C G O I V O L U M E N T O A
H B L C P H Y S I C S L N R
X U S E N S E R A J S E E C
Q Z X P A E R S M X I B U I
E Z A A G A U T P A L I Y S
N V L L B R S A L K E C G U
T Y A C O U S T I C N E T M
A E R W T I E I T E C D F I
L L M I N E R C U W E B O N
K L B G N K P Q D N O I S E
I I I E B G E R E D N U H T
N N R C T R A N S M I T D S
G G E H F D I N I Q J P M I
Y G N O S X R X G L E V E L
```

Solution on Page 339

ACT

ATTITUDE

BEHAVIOR

BLINK

BOW

CLOTHING

CODE

CUE

DANCE

EYE

FROWN

GAZE

GESTURE

GLANCES

HAND

HEAD

HUG

KINESICS

KISS

LIPS

LOOK

MESSAGE

MOTION

MOVEMENT

NOD

POINT

POSTURE

SHAKE

SHRUG

SIGN

SILENT

SMILE

STRESS

STYLE

TAP

TOUCH

VISUAL

WAVE

WINK

WRITING

```
I X S H E A D C F W S V D X
A A M L L L S H R U G P P A
A M Y K I N L O O K O O S T
M T O P M G J U W I S S O G
S B S V S I L E N T E U E L
H H L J E S E T U R C Z G I
F U M I E M Y R T H N N A J
K G L A N C E S H B A I S V
L T Q F A K I N E S D Z S W
N A C T G N I H T O L C E A
O O U U V H A N D P I X M V
D E I S E V D G E S T U R E
E D U T I T T A E D O C T K
Z C A O O V G N I T I R W A
A P R S S M I B C U Q V B H
G H S S I K N I W O B D P S
```

Solution on Page 339

AUTO

BEAM

BLACKSMITH

BRIGHT

BUILDING

BURN

CRAFT

DANGEROUS

ENERGY

EQUIPMENT

EXPERIENCE

EYE DAMAGE

FIRE

FLAMES

FLUX

FORM

FRICTION

FUSION

GLOVES

GOGGLES

HEAT

HELMET

HOT

INDUSTRY

IRON

JOINING

LASER

LIGHT

MATERIAL

MELTING

METALS

MOLTEN

SHIELD

SKILL

SOLDERING

STEEL

TORCH

TRAINING

WELD POOL

WORK

```
Y B T E M L E H E N E R G Y
R Z N N R U B U I L D I N G
T P E D E I E T O H N M I N
S A T M S M X O H O G E N I
U U L F A T P U R G N T I N
D T O I L D E I L Z I A A I
N O M R L H R E U F T L R O
I N H E E E I G L Q L S T J
Q O W A F G E A O L E E F D
T I T H U S N M B G M V L L
H T I M S K C A L B G O A E
G C T B I I E D D F R L M I
I I F S O L D E R I N G E H
R R A M N L S Y F O R M S S
B F R L A I R E T A M A E B
Q H C R O T W O R K D K Q D
```

Solution on Page 339

NAIL

NAKED

NAME

NAMING

NANNY

NAP

NARROW

NASTY

NAVAL

NAVY

NEAR

NEAT

NECK

NEED

NERVE

NEST

NET

NEVER

NEW

NEXT

NIB

NICE

NIGHT

NINE

NINTH

NOBLE

NOD

NOISE

NOISY

NONE

NOON

NOR

NOSE

NOT

NOUN

NOVEL

NOW

NURSE

NUT

NYLON

```
H P U S G Q X C E F Y N A P
D O T E N R C N L J S I G T
T G N G O E X E B E I N A J
C B Y F S Y T S O E O E N E
O Q T X E N H T N I N E E D
K P S R T I A N J E M A N U
A G A D E B W Y V A N V E N
B X N D S V O E A Y O S N M
Q M E I E H R X R D R L O P
V M C R M K R E V U A W N B
A Y K V W A A Y N V E N F R
G I N R T O N N A N A L A N
F G Y U K Y I N O I S E P O
S A N G L N G A L C N V N U
O O I O M D H N M E N O O N
B H N N T W T M D D O N W J
```

Solution on Page 340

BASE	MARCO POLO
BUILD UPS	OUT
BUSTED	PAINTBALL
CATCH	PLAY
CHASE	RECESS
CHILDHOOD	RED ROVER
CHILDREN	RUN
DOBBY	SAFE
DODGE	SCHOOL
EXERCISE	SHADOW
FAST	SPORT
FINGERS	TAG
FREEZE	TEAM
FUN	
GAME	
HAND	
HIDE	
HOME	
KIDS	
LASER	
LAUGHTER	
MANHUNT	

```
Y S O D O D G E D I H H L T
F W O D A H S X C U C W Y C
R U L V T R C E H T S A F E
T Y O A E E D R A V L H I T
I H G G A T L C S P O O D L
R U N V M H P I E M P W O U
M I C K C G R S E A O O B Y
F K W H K U L E I R H J B X
D T W B I A U N V C N B Y S
M T H R S L T S S O B U P F
I N K E E B D G P P R U F N
D U R I A C T H D O D D R T
C H I L D R E N O L R S E L
E N L T S S A S I O E T E R
G A M E A H Y U S W D A Z X
Z M S B P E B U S T E D E J
```

Solution on Page 340

ACTIVITY	LAKES
ADVENTURE	LEADER
ARTS	LEARNING
BOYS	NATURE
BUNKS	OUTDOOR
CABINS	SCOUTS
CAMPFIRES	SING
CAMPING	SONGS
CANOEING	SPORTS
CHILDREN	SUMMER
CRAFTS	SUNSHINE
DAY CAMP	SWIMMING
FISHING	TEAMS
FRIENDS	TENTS
FUN	TRAVEL
GAMES	VACATION
GIRLS	WEEK
GROUPS	WOODS
HEAT	
HIKING	
HOT	
KIDS	

```
S D W T E N T S Y O B V H L
L T C E Y T I V I T C A E E
R E D A E L N O I T A C A V
I S S M B J N J S D M Z T A
G P D S D I K K V S P U G R
S U N S H I N E N U F N N T
T O E T X U N S Y S I E I S
F R I R B T D I G E R R N G
A G R A U P G G O M E D R N
R N F R X M N N F A S L A O
C I E O O A A I I G U I E S
G K J O S C T P S M M H L P
K I T D I Y U M H S M C J O
E H O T N A R A I M E I C R
E O H U G D E C N D R X W T
W S C O U T S B G L A K E S
```

Solution on Page 340

PACE	PEN
PACK	PER
PAD	PET
PAGE	PICK
PAID	PIE
PAIL	PIG
PAIN	PILE
PAIR	PIN
PALE	PIPE
PALM	PIT
PAN	PLAN
PARK	PLAY
PART	PLOT
PASS	PLOW
PAST	POP
PAT	POT
PAW	PUB
PAY	PUT
PEA	
PEEL	
PEEP	
PEG	

```
Q E U C D I M O P Y L B G P
F L F N E A Q P I G Q P U T
Y N I K C A P I L E K T I P
A A O A A R D P E A W B I J
P K C I P I F P I A Y N T S
S X S A A A I M O E E A E E
P S L P G P A R T P R E P M
U E A Y E N A L P A T F F X
S R E P N A P L N W D L U Q
K B E P A X L Q M J N U C H
Z E C L E S O G O J M Z G Q
L V P O P G T P X N Q R R E
Z R V W Q O T O H D X A A Y
B F A V V W T Z A O P Q P H
S E Q G F J J J N G R Z E L
W Q Q U C Z W P H C Y E D L
```

Solution on Page 340

ADDRESS

ART

BABY

BIRTH

BLANK

CHRISTMAS

DESIGN

EASTER

EMOTION

ENVELOPE

EVENT

FOLDED

FRIENDS

FUNNY

GET WELL

GIFT

GLITTER

HANUKKAH

HAPPY

HOLIDAY

HUMOR

INDUSTRY

LOVE

MAIL

MESSAGE

MUSICAL

NOTE

OCCASION

PAPER

PERSONAL

PHOTO

PICTURE

SEASONAL

SEND

SMALL

SPECIAL

STAMP

SYMPATHY

THANKS

WEDDING

```
O L F H A P P Y B I R T H Z
L L S K N A H T N W J M H B
A A P M A T S D N E S M U L
I M Z H A N U K K A H A M A
C S J P Y S W E M O T I O N
E A M N T G E T W E L L R K
P Y N R O N S M U S I C A L
S U Y L G I E N V E L O P E
F E O I R G S B P E S T R Y
R V S H I S A A R T E O E A
E E C F E B P U C O A H T D
D N T R Y E T O N C S P S I
C T D T R C P E R S O N A L
S D N E I R F I T O N D E O
A C U P A L M E S S A G E H
W E D D I N G F F O L D E D
```

Solution on Page 341

A A MILNE

ADVENTURES

ANIMATION

BEAR

BOOKS

BOTHER

BRITISH

CARTOON

CHARACTERS

CHILDREN

CLASSIC

CORNER

EEYORE

FICTIONAL

FILM

FOREST

FRIENDS

GOPHER

HUNDRED ACRE

ILLUSTRATION

KANGA

OWL

PIGLET

POOHSTICKS

RABBIT

RED SHIRT

SERIES

STORIES

STUFFED

TELEVISION

TIGGER

TOYS

TREE

VIDEOS

WALT DISNEY

WINNIE

```
S L A N O I T C I F W A I N
T R S D N E I R F D A L O V
O C E E V M A F A M L I F I
I R E S T I E Y G I U T B G D
I R K C C N N L S A D E O E
E C C L S A N T M E I A P O
S A I A K E R I U E S R H S
T D T S P A N A W R N E E E
U E S S T A Z N H T E D R I
F R H I O W L H O C Y S O R
F D O C Y T S K O O B H Y E
E N O I S I V E L E T I E S
D U P E T E C H I L D R E N
L H R I U V P I G L E T A W
O O R E H T O B R E N R O C
F B R A B B I T I G G E R B
```

Solution on Page 341

ALTITUDE	MAPS
ATLAS	MOUNTAINS
BORDERS	PHYSICAL
CITIES	PROVINCES
CLIMATE	RIVERS
COASTS	SEAS
COUNTRIES	SOIL
CULTURE	STATES
DESERTS	TERRAIN
DIRECTION	TOPOGRAPHY
DISTANCE	WATER
ECOLOGY	
ECOSYSTEMS	
ENVIRONMENT	
EQUATOR	
EXPLORATION	
GEOPOLITICS	
GLACIERS	
HILLS	
LANDFORMS	
LATITUDE	
LONGITUDE	

```
S M R O F D N A L G N S E B
E E N V I R O N M E N T Q O
C D A W F B I D Q O M S U R
N U O S E I T I C P A A A D
I T D Y H P A R G O P O T E
V I W A T E R E E L S C O R
O G G V T U O C C I C O R S
R N L C E E L T O T S B M S
P O A U D T P I L I E E N D
H L C L U A X O O C T I I S
Y S I T T M E N G S A S A T
S A E U I I D Z Y T T L R R
I L R R T L T S N A S L R E
C T S E A C O U N T R I E S
A A P F L C O C D T D H T E
L I O S E M E S R E V I R D
```

Solution on Page 341

ABSTRACT	PASSION
BARCELONA	PORTRAITS
BEAUTIFUL	PRINTMAKING
BLUE PERIOD	ROSE PERIOD
CANVAS	SCULPTURE
CLASSICISM	SPANISH
CONTROVERSIAL	STUDIO
CREATIVITY	SURREALISM
CUBIST	WAR
DRAWING	WOMEN
EXPENSIVE	
EXPRESSION	
GALLERY	
HISTORY	
MASTER	
MODERN ART	
MUSEUM	
OIL	
OLD	
PAINTINGS	
PALOMA	
PARIS	

```
P A I N T I N G S I R A P T
C N E N S T I A R T R O P C
L O G B E A U T I F U L D A
A L N T W X C U B I S T G R
S E I T A S P A N I S H A T
S C K T R A N R E D O M L S
I R A Y D O I R E P E U L B
C A M B T D V Q N S F W E A
I B T D O I R E P E S O R A
S L N O L D V A R A M I Y C
M O I D U T S I W S L O O A
U Y R O T S I H T I I O W N
S B P A S S I O N A N A M V
E G E X P E N S I V E G L A
U H L Q M S I L A E R R U S
M M M A S T E R U T P L U C S
```

Solution on Page 341

ACHIEVE

CHICKEN

CHIEF

CHILD

CHIN

CHIP

CUSHION

DOLPHIN

EXHIBIT

FASHION

FISHING

HID

HIGH

HIKE

HILL

HIM

HIND

HINT

HIPS

HIRE

HIS

HIT

PUSHING

RUSHING

SHIELD

SHIFT

SHINE

SHINY

SHIP

SHIRT

SHIVER

THICK

THIEF

THIN

THIRD

THIRST

THIRTY

WHICH

WHILE

WHIP

```
W Y G Q O Q L J E T T I R D
U F Y P L J L R R F N Q I Z
B D H T F T I S S P I H D X
U G Z E R H H P U S H I N G
T I K E N I H S R E V I H S
H I K E N R H G N I H S U R
I Q F Y O S Q T H P N P P S
R A N I H T B S L T C I Z Q
D P C U S H I O N P H F A Q
X L H H L H D B O C I I S B
X Y I T I S I S I S I S E A C N
T R C H H E R P H H F T H K
T G K I C R V I S I X H I M
O J E E V I N E A G F E N H
E L N F Q G H N F H P T D W
D O N E L I H W H I P I B A
```

ADVENTURES

ANIMATION

BLUE FAIRY

BOOK

CHILDREN

CLASSIC

DISNEY

DONKEY

DREAMS

FAIRY TALE

FANTASY

FATHER

FRIENDS

HAT

ITALIAN

JIMINY CRICKET

LIES

LITERATURE

LONG NOSE

LOST

MAGIC

MARIONETTE

MISCHIEVOUS

MOVIE

MUSICAL

NOSE GROWS

NOVEL

OLD

PINOCCHIO

PLAY

PUPPETS

REAL BOY

SHOW

SON

STAR

TOY

TROUBLE

WOOD CARVER

WOODEN BOY

```
T E K C I R C Y N I M I J Y
P T L P I N O C C H I O C A
U T I A E S D M T G S D H L
P E T T T S S I O A C O I P
P N E R A Y O A S V H N L N
E O R R E L R N L N I K D O
T I A F E H I I G C E E R S
S R T A T V T A A N V Y E E
M A U N O S R A N F O R N G
A M R T Y R I A F E U L B R
E R E A L B O Y C T S T O O
R M U S I C A L N D S H O W
D A F Y O B N E D O O W K S
D G T W N O V E L B U O R T
L I E S S D N E I R F G W H
O C Y N A N I M A T I O N R
```

Solution on Page 342

AUTUMN	PERSON
BINDER	PLUCK
COMBINE	REAP
CORN	SCYTHE
CRADLE	SHEAVES
CROP	SICKLE
CUT	STALK
DARK	STRAW
DEATH	TAKE
FARM	THRESH
FIELD	TOOL
FOOD	TRACTOR
GATHER	WHEAT
GLEANING	WORK
GRAIN	
GRIM	
HAY	
IMPLEMENT	
LAND	
MACHINE	
MAIZE	
MOW	

240

```
H S T V J P H H K W X A E V
Q G K E N S E A W F S L N C
O E D L E I F O Y K K T U R
F U E R T O R D S C Y T H E
Y E H Z O K G E I U C H F L
V T N D I V D S A L O G U D
L G N I N A E L G P R E R A
E A K E B N M S B I N D E R
L A G P M M H O V I G D H C
X F B R T E O H H W A R T S
P M A G A R L C H O Z N A Q
K F D V K I A P O M M O G P
Q L E D E M N C M U G S O D
V S A O W H E A T I S R R T
P R T T O O L U X O C E I D
K R H L S D A C N V R P U M
```

Solution on Page 342

ALCOHOL

BERRY

BLACK

BUNCH

CLUSTERS

COLOR

CRUSHED

CURRANT

DRINK

EAT

EXTRACT

FERMENTED

FOOD

FRANCE

FRUITS

GRAPEVINE

GREEN

HARVEST

JAMS

JELLY

MUSCADINE

NUTRITION

PERENNIAL

PLANT

PRESS

PRODUCE

PRUNING

PURPLE

RAISINS

RIPE

SEEDLESS

SKIN

SOUR

TABLE

VARIETIES

VINEGAR

VINEYARDS

VINTAGE

WHITE

WINES

```
R V I N T A G E F R U I T S
X A H D Q P G N I N U R P E
J K G A B S R E T S U L C L
E N P E R L A I N N E R E P
L I R W N V P L A N T S T R
L R E V V I E A N G D N C U
Y D S A I C V S U E S I A P
S O S R N D I M T N E S R R
E O E I E J N N R I E I T O
N F C E Y A E B I D D A X D
I N N T A M E U T A L R E U
W I A I R S R N I C E H S C
H K R E D I G C O S S V O E
I S F S S F P H N U S L U A
T A B L E N O E R M O S R T
E F K C A L B C U R R A N T
```

Solution on Page 342

ACTION	MEDICAL
APPLIED	MORALITY
ARGUMENT	PERSONAL
ARISTOTLE	PLEASURE
BAD	POLITICS
BEHAVIOR	PROPER
BUSINESS	REAL
CODES	RELIGION
CONDUCT	RESPECT
CULTURE	RIGHT
DEATH	RULES
DECISIONS	SOCRATES
DILEMMA	STUDY
ETHICAL	THEORIES
GOOD	TRUTH
HEDONISM	VALUES
INTEGRITY	VIRTUE
JUDGMENT	
JUSTICE	
LAW	
LIFE	
LOVE	

```
A R Y D U T S E U T R I V S
N R E B I T S D J L I F E Y
Q O G L U L S E U L A V T M
S T I U I S E X D Y A I H E
W R T T M G I M G N R W I D
S U M C C E I N M G U D C I
O T O E U A N O E A L E A C
C H R P L D S T N S E R L A
R E A S T T N C T C S U M L
A O L E U I O O I U C S G D
T R I R R D I T C T I A R E
E I T V E D S H S N I E E I
S E Y S A U I D O I A L V L
J S H B J H C D O L R P O P
R E P O R P E R S O N A L P
E D E A T H D B T H G I R A
```

Solution on Page 343

BASS

BOW

CELLO

CLASSICAL

CONCERT

CORD

CURVED

DRAW

EXPENSIVE

FIDDLE

FROG

GRIP

GUITAR

HAIR

HAND

IVORY

LONG

MUSIC

NOTE

PERFORMANCE

PLAY

PLUCK

PRACTICE

PULL

RESIN

ROSIN

SMOOTH

SOUND

STICK

STRUM

SYMPHONY

TECHNIQUE

TENSION

TONE

VIBRATION

VIOLA

WAX

WOOD

246

```
Y G E N K W D B L B O W M W
F S T I C K O X D Y N O M D
E U M S T E N S I O N O U F
P C E O F R O G R I P D T J
J L N R O L E L D D I F E E
P A A A A T N C W P L U C K
P S S Y M P H O N Y U Z H D
E S V I B R A T I O N P N R
R I A H Y R O V I N C U I O
F C X L O N G F L I O L Q C
T A P S T R U M R S U L U D
W L S C E V I S N E P X E K
A A E E C I T C A R P V N O
B I A L G O A T W A R D O V
Y K S L W L R N D U D E T H
M T S O H A N D C I S U M Q
```

Solution on Page 343

ABSTRACT	PALETTE
ALFRED SISLEY	PERCEPTION
ANGLES	PERIOD
ART MOVEMENT	PORTRAITS
ARTISTS	STYLE
CANVAS	SUBJECTIVE
CLAUDE MONET	VAN GOGH
COLOR	VISUAL ARTS
COMPOSITION	
DEGAS	
EXHIBITION	
IMAGES	
IMPASTO	
LANDSCAPES	
LE CHARIVARI	
LIGHT	
LITERATURE	
LOUIS LEROY	
MARY CASSATT	
OIL	
PAINTERS	
PAINTINGS	

```
S U B J E C T I V E L Y T S
Z N S T I A R T R O P I L L
A N G L E S C U P A C O L I
C O L O R A T A I L T A E G
V I A V R A L N A S L N C H
I T A T R E T U A F I O H T
S I S E T I D P R Y O I A T
U B T T N E M E V O M T R A
A I E G M I D R A R S I I S
L H S O M S A C N E R S V S
A X N A I R A E G L E O A A
R E G S T N A P O S T P R C
T E L I V O C T G I N M I Y
S E S A G E D I H U I O P R
Y T S P E R I O D O A C G A
S E P A C S D N A L P U E M
```

Solution on Page 343

RACE	RIBS
RACK	RICE
RAFT	RICH
RAG	RID
RAID	RIM
RAIL	RING
RAIN	RINK
RAKE	RIPE
RAM	RISE
RAN	RISK
RARE	ROAD
RAT	ROAM
RAW	ROB
RAY	ROD
READ	ROW
REAL	RUB
REAR	RUG
RED	RUN
REED	
RELY	
RENT	
REST	

```
D U E G P R E K A R A C E J
J Y S B I R E N T R A F T R
O S A N A R I D V A L C O O
B C K R I P A R A I N A K W
P F A M F F I T A D D Q E O
E J Y L C S R R S A R E A R
C H R O K R O B R E L Y R H
C P W A M A D E E R R I C E
R J K G M N P S R A N I K Y
V P B D G B Q Q A G R A W A
U Y C O B R T H U N I I E W
T C S Y L B F R N T S Z P D
I F M X H V X U W D E Z W E
U L B A J Q A N U S Z R V R
R X X H V V Z O I D M A K U
R Z F K Z L E V A K R L O B
```

Solution on Page 343

ACID

ARABICA

AROMA

BARISTA

BATCH

BEAN

BITTER

BLACK

BLEND

BODY

BOLD

BRAZIL

BREW

BROWN

BURNT

CAFE

COFFEE

COLOR

COOLING

CUP

DARK

DRY

FILTER

FIRE

FLAVOR

FRESH

FULL

GREEN

GRIND

HEAT

HOT

JAVA

LIGHT

MEDIUM

OVEN

POT

PRESS

ROAST

SMELL

TASTE

```
H G S T N P Z G W I X N B N
W S S E A P U J S M E F L C
S H E E F F O C T V C I M M
J R R R K F B R O W N R B X
G C P B F C R X J B R E W R
I D O O G U A D N I R G H W
F U L L E N Z L I T A C D R
M Y R D O Z I W B T R K F O
T H G I L R L L S E A N E A
Y C X B T O P I O R B F N S
S T R H E V R L D O I H O T
H A M O R A L B W L C P N A
J B G K B L N L T D A R K E
T A S T E F M E D I U M L H
Z T V M F P R N D B O D Y J
O D S A K A I D I C A F E X
```

Solution on Page 344

ALPHABET

ANCIENT

ARTIST

ASIAN

BEAUTIFUL

BLACK

CHINESE

CREATIVE

CURSIVE

DECORATIVE

DELICATE

DESIGNS

DOCUMENTS

DRAWING

ELEGANT

EXPRESSIVE

FLOURISH

FONTS

GOTHIC

HANDWRITING

INK BRUSH

LANGUAGE

MANUSCRIPT

NAMES

NIB

PAPER

PARCHMENT

PENMANSHIP

PRACTICE

ROMAN

SERIF

STYLES

TYPOGRAPHY

VISUAL ART

WORDS

```
E T A C I L E D E S I G N S
G N I D O C U M E N T S P R A
A E B Q W O G F F A S I A N U
U I E F L O U R I S H T R I G
G C E Z T E R E R T Y E C B N
N N V H P V V D E I U B H I A
A A I T P I R C S U N A M N L
L C S T T T H D R T F H E K P
C S A I A R S R O Y P N B R U
E N K R O A N A M L T R A R R
A C O W T L A W A E U C S P M
A C S D F A M I N S T I X E L
E G A N T U N N H I V E S B D
R E P A P S E G C E T Y P O G
R A P H Y I P E S E N I H C A
R T I S T V
```

Solution on Page 344

ACTRESS	MUSICIAN
ALBUMS	OOPS
AMERICAN	PAPARAZZI
ARTIST	PERFUME
AWARDS	POP STAR
BLOND	POPULAR
CELEBRITY	PREGNANT
CHILDREN	PRETTY
CIRCUS	RECORD
COMEBACK	SCANDAL
CONCERT	SEXY
DANCER	SHAVE
DIVORCED	SHOW
DRUGS	SISTER
FAMOUS	SONS
FANS	TEEN
JIVE	TOUR
KIDS	VIDEO
LOUISIANA	
MEDIA	
MOTHER	
MTV	

Britney Spears

```
W S Y F Y R E V A H S D I K
O O A I D E M U F R E P O T
H N S I S T E R E H T O M O
S S T N A N G E R P L P R U
M U S I C I A N T A O S Y R
X B L O N D G M E P U T C E
A C T R E S S C E A I A O C
D I V O R C E D N R S R M O
A W A R D S N S B A I S E R
P O P U L A R E J Z A C B D
T O E D I V L X I Z N A A A
D S Z B H E P Y V I A N C N
S Z I I C O N C E R T D K C
P R E T T Y S M U B L A K E
O S U C R I C M T V B L M R
O F C J F A M O U S G U R D
```

Solution on Page 344

ASIA	JUICE
BEET	MACHETE
BOILING	MILL
CANE	MOLASSES
CARIBBEAN	PERENNIAL
COMBINE	PLANT
COOKING	PURE
CROP	RAW
CUBA	REED
CULTIVATE	REFINE
CUTTING	RUM
ETHANOL	SPECIES
FIBROUS	STOUT
FIELD	SUGAR
FOOD	SWEET
GROW	TALL
HARVEST	TROPICS
HAWAII	WATER
HEAT	
HYBRIDS	
INDUSTRY	
ISLANDS	

```
N W W W W A T E R F I E L D
T Y A O Y Z W T R E Z T V Q
A A T R E E D H A R V E S T
L M E G B B Y A G U C H K U
L U E H N O F N U P U C C O
H A W A I I I O S I T A J T
W E S R W B K L O X T M H S
S P E C I E S O I D I T Y E
Y R T S U D N I O N N E B N
P N A E B B I R A C G E R I
L P V S C T I S U O R B I F
L A I N N E R E P M P N D E
I R T A A O P C U B A O S R
M O L A S S E S C I P O R T
U P U C I I S L A N D S X C
R E C C A J U I C E N A C X
```

Solution on Page 344

ADVANTAGE

ARCHIMEDES

AXLE

BASIC

BUILDING

CHANGES

CLOCK

DEVICE

DIRECTION

EASY

ELEMENTARY

ENERGY

ENGINEER

EQUILIBRIUM

FORCE

FRICTION

GEAR

HELPFUL

IDEA

INCLINE

INVENTION

LEVER

LOAD

MAGNITUDE

MECHANICS

MOVEMENT

OUTPUT

PHYSICS

PIVOT

PLANE

POWER

PULLEY

SCREW

TORQUE

USEFUL

VECTOR

WEDGE

WHEEL

WORK

```
K C H A N G E S C I S Y H P
R E V E L E M E N T A R Y L
Y D H A M E G D W U V K A A
R E E N I G N E E S M C C N
D V L A E D I M R E W O P E
J I P L E E D I C F M L S E
R C F I U W L H S U E C N T
A E U N Q P I C I L I E G N
D W L V R I U R X N R N O E
V H O E O B B A A G V I U M
A E A N T I A H Y E T L T E
N E D T L E C S C C G C P V
T L D I R E C T I O N N U O
A E U O M W O R K C E I T M
G Q Q N W R F T O V I P Q S
E D U T I N G A M F Y S A E
```

Solution on Page 345

BACKWARDS

BLADES

BONFIRE

COATS

COLD

DANCE

EARMUFFS

FALLING

FRIENDS

FUN

GLIDING

GLOVES

HAT

HELMET

JACKET

JUDGES

JUMPS

LACES

LAKE

LEGGINGS

LEOTARD

LESSONS

MEDALS

MITTENS

MOVES

MUSIC

OLYMPICS

RACE

SCARVES

SKILL

SLIPPERY

SNOW

SPINS

SPORT

SWEATER

TUMBLES

TURNS

TWIRLING

WINTER

ZAMBONI

```
L S P O R T J S N O S S E L
N L F S A A G N I L L A F S
A N I E C N A D O I C U D E
X M S K E F K L P O N R S D
Q I E S S J Y P L A K E I A
T T V G D M E D A L S T N L
U T R N P R G E R I F N O B
R E A I Y L A N J D F I B O
N N C G S P A W I U U W M U
S S S G L E J C K L M M A S
C D H E H I V M E C R P Z W
I N E L G E D O O S A I S E
S E L B M U T I L V E B W A
U I M C O A T S N G E X O T
M R E E R A J U D G E S N E
R F T D H B S P I N S V S R
```

Solution on Page 345

BAMBOO STRAW

BEND

BEVERAGE

CHEAP

CHILDREN

COCKTAIL

COMMON

CONTAINER

CRAZY

CUP

DATE

DISPOSABLE

DRINK

FLEXIBLE

FUN

GLASS

HOLLOW

JUICE

KIDS

LID

MILK

MOUTH

PAPER

POLYPROPYLENE

RESTAURANT

SANITARY

SHORT

SIP

SLURP

SODA

SPOON STRAW

STIR

STRAIGHT

STRIPED

SUCK

TUBE

WATER

WRAPPED

```
V P R U L S D I K L I M P J
F U N U H K O C O M M O N L
H C B O F L E X I B L E J L
S T R A I G H T Y Y Y T S I
V T U D M I V R P S R A P U
D Z L O E B E R A S E D O W
I E L I M P O N C A S I O X
K D P M A P I O B L T S N C
S N P P Y T N R S G A P S W
W E I L A T K P T T U O T L
A B E R A R K C U S R S R R
T N Y I D C W S O D A A A J
E V N E R D L I H C N B W U
R E G A R E V E B U T L S I
R R Z P I S T I R P A E H C
A Y P Z B Q H O L L O W L E
```

Solution on Page 345

ANCHOR

BINDING

CHAIN

CLIMBING

DECORATIVE

DOUBLE

FISHERMEN

FRAY

GRANNY

HITCH

JOINING

LACE

LINK

LOOSE

MARITIME

MAST

MATERIAL

NAUTICAL

OVERHAND

ROPES

SAILORS

SCOUTS

SECURING

SHIPS

SKILL

SLIP

SQUARE

STRENGTH

STRING

STRONG

TENT

TIES

TIGHT

TOGETHER

TWIST

TYING

WEAVING

WEBBING

WHIP

YARN

```
E C A L L B R W H I P T A R R
R S R O L I A S T R O N G T
A E U L I N H T Y I N G J I
U U H A K D R T F L O O S E
Q E H T S I E A G R I M C S
S F I K E N L N Y N A W N C
X I T N T G I A I R E Y A O
E S C I S V O N I B O R U U
L H H L A P G T B R V G T T
B E Z E I L I I R R E P I S
U R W L G M N H G O R T C L
O M S A E G B F S R H H A O
D E C O R A T I V E A C L M
G N I R U C E S N I N N N S
R O P E S T R I N G D U N A
P T S I W T I G H T S A M Y
```

Solution on Page 345

AIR	OPEN
AWNING	ORIEL
BAY	OUTSIDE
BLIND	PANE
CAR	PICTURE
CHURCH	PLASTIC
CLEAN	SASH
CLOSE	SCREEN
CRACK	SEAL
DESIGN	SHADES
DISPLAY	SHUT
DOOR	SILL
DOUBLE	SOLAR
DRAPES	SUN
FRAME	TINTED
FRENCH	VIEW
GLASS	VINYL
GRIDS	WALL
HOUSE	
LIGHT	
LOCK	
METAL	

```
S E P A R D F S I L L Q D N
P D A L K C H A D A D T E Z
D I S P L A Y S H O D P S Y
R S C H U R C H S O O H Z A
A R T I T Y Y N D A L U R Z H
D U T E U E I K A T B S S W
W O S N S R I T D G L D E J
Y A A O G V E E J W E I A N
M O L W A M T Y B S V N L F
L C P L N N D N I L B V A V
T Y D S I I E G L S Z F C P
C T N T H C N E R F S R S L
T H G I L A I G R K A A O Y
K S Y E V R D U P C U M L H
Z U A R O I M E K O S E A G
U N B E L P K H S L C A R W
```

Solution on Page 346

BOW	ROPE
BREEZE	SAIL
CANVAS	SCHOONER
CAPTAIN	SEA
CATAMARAN	SHIP
CLIMB	SPAR
CREW	SPEED
DECK	STERN
FORE	TALL
HOIST	TIMBER
JIGGER	TOP
KETCH	TRAVEL
LINES	VERTICAL
LOWER	WATER
MAIN	WIND
MIZZEN	WOOD
OCEAN	YACHT
POLE	YAWL
PORT	
RACING	
RADAR	
RIG	

```
S Z M F S H I P O T V Q G Z
Y S T O R A P S E A D O S R
A W T R H Y V B E G E O Y E
W N C E O E A N E Y E C T T
L I A S R P P C A G P E R A
R G P R E N O O H C S A Y W
D T T B A L Y P R T V N T P
B D A N M M I Z Z E N I A M
G N I C A R A P L J Z J L D
D I N B V E R T I C A L L O
Q W O J Z A I G A R I P Z O
Y W I E D M G X E C S K V W
O E E A B E J W L P E C U R
J R R E R H O I S T N E F S
B C R I C L M R C H I D W O
L W G L G B E H P O L E Q A
```

Solution on Page 346

BAKING

BEET SUGAR

BROWN SUGAR

CAKES

CALORIES

CANE SUGAR

CEREAL

CONFECTIONER

COOKIES

CRYSTALLINE

DESSERT

FLAVOR

FOOD

FRUCTOSE

GLUCOSE

HONEY

ICING

INGREDIENT

INSULIN

LACTOSE

MOLASSES

OBESITY

PIE

POWDERED

PROCESSED

RAW

REFINING

SUGAR BEET

SUGAR CUBES

SUGARCANE

SWEETNESS

SYRUPS

TEA

TOOTH DECAY

Sugary Sweet

```
Y T I S E B O S Y R U P S Y
G L U C O S E I K O O C B D
F B E R A G U S N W O R B N
O D E S S E R T D N A Y E I
O I T H O A T E F G S S E L
D N S O W T R E U X E T T U
E G W N O E C S A B S A S S
S R E E D T E U U M S L U N
S E E Y I N H C R D A L G I
E D T O A O R D X F L I A F
C I N C L A E R E C O N R L
O E E O G N I C I C M E C A
R N S U S E I R O L A C A V
P T S U G A R B E E T Y N O
I B A K I N G N I N I F E R
E W D L L A C T O S E K A C
```

Solution on Page 346

PUZZLES • 273

ADVENTURES

ANIMATION

BERT

BOOKS

BRITISH

BROADWAY

CAROUSEL

CARPETBAG

CHILDREN

CLASSIC

COCKNEY

DANCING

ENGLISH

FANTASY

FATHER

FLOATING

HAPPY

JANE

KITE

LONDON

MAGIC

MICHAEL

MOVIE

MR BANKS

MUSICAL

NANNY

P L TRAVERS

PENGUINS

SINGING

SONGS

STAGE

SUFFRAGETTE

TEA PARTY

TUPPENCE

UMBRELLA

WALT DISNEY

```
H L A C I S U M R E H T A F
S K O O B R I T I S H M K A
I S C H I L D R E N G I G N
L O A L L E R B M U T C Y T
G N R S N I U G N E P H A A
N G O Y E N S I D T L A W S
E S U F F R A G E T T E D Y
O T S L B O D A N Y R L A E
G E E O E Y V M O N A E O N
N A L A R P E A D N V G R K
I P E T T P N G N A E A B C
C A N I M A T I O N R T D O
N R A N G H U C L A S S I C
A T J G C A R P E T B A G A
D Y T U P P E N C E I V O M
G N I G N I S K N A B R M D
```

Solution on Page 346

ANALYSIS

ANCIENT

ARCHITECTURE

ARTIFACTS

BIOFACTS

BONES

BURIED

CITY

DATA

DESERT

DIGGING

DISCOVERY

DUST

EGYPT

EXCAVATION

EXPLORE

GROUND

HISTORICAL

IRON AGE

LANDSCAPES

MUMMY

OLD

PAINSTAKING

PRESERVATION

RECOVERY

REMAINS

RESEARCH

ROME

SAND

SCIENTISTS

SITES

STONE AGE

STUDY

SURVEYANCE

TREASURE

UNCOVER

```
S E N O B I O F A C T S U D
S T U D Y R E V O C N U A L
G N O I T A V R E S E R P O
E R U S A E R T N J C V A A
X L D C I T Y T O H F E N N
P A I N S T A K I N G Y C A
L N S V T L R T T F R A I L
O D C G S A E D A T A N E Y
R S O R I C C D V H E C N S
E C V O T I O I A C G E T I
M A E U N R V G C R A O P S
A P R N E O E G X A N E Y A
I E Y D I T R I E E O M G N
N S Z Z C S Y N A S R O E D
S E T I S I D G D E I R U B
Y M M U M H E W T R E S E D
```

Solution on Page 347

GAIN	GOD
GALE	GOES
GAME	GOLD
GANG	GOLF
GAP	GONE
GAS	GOOD
GATE	GOT
GAVE	GRAB
GAY	GRAN
GAZE	GRAY
GEAR	GREW
GERM	GRIM
GET	GRIN
GIFT	GRIP
GIN	GUM
GIRL	GUN
GIVE	GUY
GLAD	GYM
GLOW	
GLUE	
GOAL	
GOAT	

```
M Q F G U Y E M A G A L E L
M B G A R E N M A A Q T P E
W L E P R I N I E N G A Z E
A B T N G H N U V G A T E G
K I L Z O R L N I N V T R L
G Z S E O G D F G G E A R O
O F A T X R T U O E B I F W
D R V N M A N L D R G L A D
L S G S D N D E U M O O Y G
K A B N Q V M X T G A Y A G
G V D F U V P Z O R T S R L
M R N G F G G O G I K E G C
N K V Y E R D Y U M W B R T
Q I O E N F L C M A D E I F
V S O V T W U J Q K B C P U
R N M Z O T E H G K E T U L
```

Solution on Page 347

AMERICAN

ARTISTIC

BRIDGES

BUILDINGS

CITIES

COLORS

COOL

CREATIVE

CRIME

DAMAGE

DEFACING

DESIGNS

GANGS

ILLEGAL

IMAGES

KIDS

LETTERS

MARKERS

MESSAGES

MURALS

NAMES

PAINTING

PICTURES

POLICE

PUBLIC

SIGNATURE

STREET

STYLES

SUBWAYS

SYMBOLS

TAGGING

TALENT

TERRITORY

TRAINS

UGLY

URBAN

WALLS

WRITING

```
C L T S Y A W B U S K S P D
O N A B R U X G U E Q G P A L
L P L G K E N C N G G N I M
O O E B E I T I A A N I C A R
R L N N C L D T M M I D T G
S I T A M G L S E I G L U E
E C F C I N W I S L G I R A
G E S I I I C T S N A U E X
D G Y R O T I R R E T B S S
I N M E Y N I A E A L N L E
R I B M L I M E N A G Y T G
B T O A G A N G S I T E T A
C I L B U P I D S O E I Y S
O R S A L S R E K R A M V S
O W A L L S D U T C R I M E
L C T R A I N S S L A R U M
```

Solution on Page 347

ARCH

BOOT

BRAND

CLOG

COLOR

COMFORT

CROCS

CUSHION

FASHION

FEET

FIT

FOOT

GALOSHES

GARMENT

HEEL

HIKE

HOSIERY

LACES

LEG

LOAFER

MATERIAL

MOCCASIN

NIKE

PUMPS

RUBBER

RUNNING

SANDAL

SHOE

SIZE

SLIPPER

SNEAKER

SOCK

SPORTS

STRAP

SUPPORT

TENNIS

TOE

WALK

WARMTH

WOOD

```
O S E C A L E G Z P U M P S
E O N S Y T R O F M O C P S
A F N E Y N I S A C C O M G
Y H A H A R D T G F R O G W
N E N S E K E Y M T D A V B
C E K O H R E I S A R C H O
Q L S L I I I U R S M T I I O
A S O A A H O N E O K E R T
O U L G N W S N N E H U E W
B P J I H D T U T I B N O F
M P R D P T A K C B N O H O
U O O P U P M L E I D G S O
E R L O A F E R S N I K E T
X T O G A R O R A W C C Z I
W S C O R C T R V W V O I F
S C K L H B B S K G M S S J
```

Solution on Page 347

ACTOR	MOONWALK
ALBUMS	MOTOWN
ARTIST	MTV
BAD	MUSICIAN
BEAT IT	NEWS
BLACK	NOSE
BROTHERS	PEPSI
BUBBLES	PRINCE
CELEBRITY	RICH
CHILD	ROCK
CONCERTS	SINGING
COURT	STAR
DANCING	SURGERY
EPIC	THRILLER
FAMILY	TITO
FAMOUS	TOUR
GRAMMY	TRIAL
HISTORY	VIDEOS
ICON	
INDIANA	
JERMAINE	
LAWSUIT	

```
I R O T C A C N K S T V D K
R I C H H I S T O R Y I A D
D K I K P R D M A S V D B B
K L L E C A I N U Y E E C T
D C O A N O A L M B A O O B
M P A C W I R M L T L S U Q
E U I L D N A C I E C A R S
X N S N B R O T H E R S T L
G Y I I G N V O L Q X A I A
V A C A C T S E M C R Q U I
N O R E M I B U B B L E S R
N W R T N R A P R E J P W T
I T O G I N E N H G E D A I
S U I T E S B J H P E A L T
R N Y W O K T E C N I R P O
G H S U O M A F A M I L Y U
```

Solution on Page 348

ANARCHY

ANGER

BANDS

BASS

BRITISH

CONCERTS

COOL

DANCE

DRUMS

EMO

ENGLAND

FASHION

GENRE

GOTH

GREEN DAY

GUITARS

HAIR

HARD CORE

LEATHER

LONDON

LOUD

LYRICS

MOHAWK

MOSH

NEW WAVE

NEW YORK

PIERCINGS

POLITICAL

RADIO

REBEL

ROCK MUSIC

SCREAMING

SEATTLE

SONGS

STYLE

TATTOOS

THE CLASH

VIOLENT

WILD

YOUTHFUL

```
D R U M S P O D N A L G N E
W I H S I T I R B Y R E O M
J P P Z L R I E R G W C D T
S T Y L E A K I R Y D N N A
G E S B H W C E O C L A O T
N C E C A S E R C O I D L T
O L O H R N K E K O W N E O
S I O N D E D O M L G P G O
M M D A C U A S U H O F U S
V L Y A O E Y M S L T A I E
I E Z L R B R H I D H S T A
O A N G E R A T C N G H A T
L T H S O M I S S R G I R T
E H T H E C L A S H A O S L
N E W W A V E M O G E N R E
T R A L U F H T U O Y S A V
```

Solution on Page 348

ANGELIC

ART

BEAUTIFUL

BEINGS

BIBLE

CHERUB

CHILDREN

CHURCH

CLOUDS

COMFORT

DIVINE

ETERNAL

FLOAT

FLYING

GABRIEL

GOOD

GOWN

GUIDANCE

HALO

HEAVENLY

HERALD

HOLY

JESUS

KIND

LORD

LOVE

MERCY

MICHAEL

MIRACLES

MUSIC

PROTECT

PURE

ROBES

SHOULDER

SING

SWEET

TRUMPET

WHITE

WINGS

WISE

```
O S N V D H C L F J E S U S
H R F M A F A W I N G S H W
P Y L L I N Y O C N D M E E
U B O C R C G M I L S C R E
R U A E R O H E U E O H A T
R T E O M B A L S H U L W
V E M D S F R C E I I R D I
O H C I T O A R T L C C O S
L C N H B R E D L U O H S E
P G U E I T C E T O R P W L
U N S M Y L N E V A E H E B
Y I E C N A D I U G I I N I
Y Y T E P M U R T T R K I B
V L U F I T U A E B I P V F
R F O M B W F Q A N A D I N
V E A H N W O G D L O R D D
```

Solution on Page 348

ANTIFREEZE

APARTMENT

AUTOMOBILE

BOILER

BUILDING

CAP

CENTRAL

CIRCULATE

COILS

COLD

CONVECTOR

COOL

COPPER

CORE

DEVICE

ELECTRIC

ENERGY

ENGINE

EXCHANGE

FAN

FLUID

GRILLE

HEAT

HOT

IRON

LIQUID

METAL

PIPE

PUMP

RADIATION

STEAM

TEMPERATURE

THERMAL

TRANSFER

TUBES

VEHICLE

WARMTH

WATER

WINTER

Radiator

```
Z Z T C M B T N D N S C T A
E R O C O I L S O I C O L D
E E N I G N E R F M U O Y I
E L L Z I C I R T C E L E U
Y E L I B O M O T U A T F Q
R G R I T N E M T R A P A I
E N R U R I Z U E L R E T L
P A E E T G E T U B E S H A
P H T P N A E C I F T W E R
O C A I P E R E F S N A R T
C X W P A I F E L L I R M N
D E V I C E I A P C W M A E
C O N V E C T O R M I T L C
B U I L D I N G T A E H O P
V F R A D I A T I O N T E H
P M A E T S F E C P U M P V
```

Solution on Page 348

PUZZLES • 291

ARTICLES	POLITICS
AUTHOR	POSTS
BLOGGER	RANT
COMMENTS	READERS
COMPUTER	SEARCH
CONTENT	SHORT
DAILY	STORY
FORUM	SUBJECT
GOSSIP	TALK
IMAGES	TOPICS
INTERNET	TWITTER
KEYBOARD	TYPE
LIFE	UPDATE
LINKS	VENT
MEDIA	VIDEOS
NEWS	WEBLOG
OPINIONS	WEBSITE
PEOPLE	WRITING
PERSONAL	
PHOTOS	
PICTURES	
PODCAST	

```
V T R O H S G N I T I R W E
S O E D I V Y R O T S O E L
U P D A T E P Y T N T H B P
I I H A A F F O R U M T S O
T C C O M M E N T S S U I E
V S C O M P U T E R E A T P
M E D I A S N L N L G S E I
T A N N O A C S A D A C C C
A R K T R I G N K C M I O T
L C O E T E O O D N I T N U
K H F R Y S T O S V I I T R
P I A N R B P T Y S N L E E
L S W E N C O P I N I O N S
J T P T Y L I A D W U P T I
W E B L O G G E R S T S O P
T C E J B U S R E D A E R P
```

Solution on Page 349

AFRICAN

AMAZON

ANIMAL

BEAK

BILL

BIRDS

BLUE

BRIGHT

CAGE

COLORS

CREST

EGGS

EXOTIC

FEATHERS

FLIGHT

FOOD

FRUIT

GREEN

LARGE

LEARNING

LOUD

MACAWS

MATE

MIMIC

NECTAR

PERCH

PETS

REPEAT

SEEDS

SINGING

SPECIES

STRONG

TALKING

TOYS

TREES

TRICKS

WATER

WILD

WORDS

ZOOS

```
X W U J H D U O L Z S E B C
H A H C O L O R S W X W A B
S T R O S T E N T O O G U E
A E F M P F E A T H E R S G
P R A O E N F I R G G K D G
L U N M C R C J Q N C I D S
A Q I A I G W B F I I Y L B
R D M C E F I B R G R N E F
G C A A S R L T R N L A G C
E N L W D T D G N I K L A T
U T O S R W E S O S G E I F
L Z R R N E D P Z G T H R B
B Z A E T E P L A A F U T I
F O X Y E S E E M C I M I M
T O Y S Y S R R A T C E N Y
N S I P P G M K G T S E R C
```

Solution on Page 349

ANIMALS

AQUARIUM

AQUATIC

ATTACKS

BEACH

BITE

BLOOD

BULL

CAGE

CARNIVOROUS

CARTILAGE

CONSERVATION

DANGEROUS

FEAR

FLORIDA

FOOD

GILLS

GREAT WHITE

HAMMERHEAD

HUNTER

INTELLIGENT

KILL

LARGE

NURSE

OCEANS

PLANKTON

PREDATOR

REEF

ROWS OF TEETH

SEAWATER

SNOUT

SPIRACLE

SWIMMING

TAIL

TIGER SHARK

TOOTH

VERTEBRATE

Solution on Page

```
H K F I A H E L C A R I P S
C T E N Q S E A W A T E R W
A E E T U A T T A C K S E I
E G R E A T W H I T E K D M
B A V L T Z W C D V R A A M
B C E L I F O O D A E N T I
T I R I C U O N H H T I O N
U B T G I L L S R T N M R G
O U E E B I R E W O U A L O
N L B N A E M R G O H L A C
S L R T G M D V Z T R S R E
Z I A I A Q U A R I U M G A
R K T H C A R T I L A G E N
A U E C A R N I V O R O U S
E P L A N K T O N U R S E R
F L O R I D A N G E R O U S
```

Solution on Page 349

ACADEMICS

ART

BOOKS

CHILDREN

CLASSES

COLLEGE

COMPUTERS

DEBT

DEGREE

DIPLOMA

DISTRICTS

ENGLISH

EXAMS

EXPENSIVE

FAILING

FEDERAL

FREE

FUNDING

GRADES

HEALTH

HISTORY

LOANS

LOCAL

MATH

PRIVATE

PROGRAMS

PUBLIC

READING

RECESS

REQUIRED

SCHOOL

SCIENCE

STATE

STUDY

SUMMER

TEACHER

TEST

TUITION

UNIONS

WRITING

```
L S N A O L A R E D E F L U S
S E F A I L I N G I T M O N R
R C O M P U T E R S A S O I I
G N I D A E R R E T V T H O N
N E H M I A L D H R I A C N S
I I E S E P O L C I R T S S S
T C A M V D C I A C P E R S S
I S L A I H A H E T S E T E R
R U T X S W L C T S Q G Z C E
W M H E N M D R A U N E I E I
B M I N E I A L I I T L G R E
O E S G P R C R D E B L R S T
O R T L X B E N G U E O A T L
K A O I E D U H P O D C D U E
S M R S A F R E E E R G E D U
A X Y H T U I T I O N P S Y
```

Solution on Page 349

ADJUST	MAGNETIC
AERIAL	NOISE
AIR	POLE
ALUMINUM	PORTABLE
AMPLITUDE	POWER
ANALOG	RADAR
BANDWIDTH	RECEIVE
CAR	SIGNAL
CHANNEL	SOUND
CONDUCTOR	STATIC
CURRENT	TALK
DEVICE	TOWER
DIRECTION	TRANSMIT
ELECTRIC	TUNE
ELEMENTS	VEHICLE
EQUIPMENT	VOLTAGE
EXTEND	WAVE
FOLDING	WIRE
FREQUENCY	
HERTZ	
IMPEDANCE	
LONG	

```
R F L N C C E G A T L O V T
D J O O O P H C D I M S W O
B E E L N I C A O M A I I W
G L V Q D G T I N S G G R E
T O I I U I K C T N N N E R
U P M H C I N L E A E A W A
N D P E T E P G A R T L O D
E R E R O D C M O T I S P A
L A D T R M I I E L C D O R
E C A Z E V A W R N A G R E
M U N I M U L A D T T N T V
E R C F R E Q U E N C Y A I
N R E D U T I L P M A E B E
T E X T E N D N U O S B L C
S N O I S E V E H I C L E E
P T S U J D A E R I A L B R
```

Solution on Page 350

BAMBOO	LOOP
BLOOD	LOOSE
BOOK	MOOD
BOOM	MOON
BOOT	MOOSE
BROOK	NOON
CHOOSE	POOL
COOK	POOR
COOL	ROOF
CUCKOO	ROOM
DOOR	ROOT
FLOOD	SHOOT
FLOOR	SOON
FOOD	SPOON
FOOL	TOO
FOOT	WOOD
GOOD	WOOL
GOOSE	ZOO
HOOK	
HOOP	
LOOK	
LOOM	

```
G P I F N Q N E V F O Y M F
J L D Q L O S K W R W S Y Z
M X M O D O O L B O Z O O W
T O O H O O O P O O H P O C
C S O G C K F R S T O O A L
E S S N V C W O P V D T Y T
F S E V H U O L O O K E P M
K L T O C C D O O R N O M N
D O O B M A B G L O O M V H
R S O O O M M K O L O O L V
E L H R D O O D O D N Y M U
E E S T B O K O F O O T X W
L C P S H B O O T P O O R P
Q G G J B T V F W W S L M H
N A P S E Y V D M C J R O W
H C N C X B B B U Q I D Q Y
```

Solution on Page 350

ANIMALIA

ASP

BITE

CARNIVOROUS

CHORDATA

COBRA

COIL

CORAL SNAKE

COTTONMOUTH

DANGEROUS

DESERT

EDEN

EGG

EYES

FANGS

FORKED TONGUE

GARDEN

GARTER SNAKE

JAW

LONG

MEDICINE

MOULTING

PET

PIT

POISONOUS

PYTHONS

RATTLESNAKE

REPTILIA

SCALES

SHED

SIDEWINDING

SKIN

SLIMY

SQUAMATA

TEETH

VENOMOUS

WATER

ZOO

```
Z W Y T L O N G H T E E T P
E Y E S C A L E S G T J R O
E N I C I D E M D A I A E I
S U O R E G N A D R B W S S
E G G A R T E R S N A K E O
C A R N I V O R O U S G D N
V N J C O R A L S N A K E O
E I G N I T L U O M P D J U
N M R G N I D N I W E D I S
O A E K A N S E L T T A R A
M L P P S A L S K I N J Z J
O I T L C I C H O R D A T A
U A I C O T T O N M O U T H
S M L C B D Z S G N A F B H
Y T I P R E T A W D E H S W
A T A M A U Q S N O H T Y P
```

Solution on Page 350

BABY GRAND

BACH

BEETHOVEN

BLACK

CHOPIN

CHORDS

COMPOSERS

CONCERTO

EBONY

GRAND PIANO

HAMMERS

INSTRUMENT

IVORIES

JAZZ

KEYBOARD

MELODY

MOZART

MUSICIAN

NOTES

OCTAVE

ORGAN

PEDALS

PERCUSSION

PERFORMANCE

PIANIST

PIANOFORTE

PRACTICE

SCALES

SCORES

SHARP

SOLO

STEINWAY

STRINGS

UPRIGHT

WHITE

WOOD

```
P Y S G N I R T S D R O H C
I N S T R U M E N T B J W H
A O O S H A R P T R A Z O M
N B L I E G N D S Z B O O P
I E M O S I I D Z L Y T D E
S Y E H S S R R P P G R P D
T A L C Q A U O P I R E E A
B W O A O N B C V U A C R L
L N D B C A E Z R I N N F S
A I Y O T I E B S E D O O C
C E P R A C T I C E P C R A
K T E U V I H W H I T E M L
Y S S R E S O P M O C O A E
N A G R O U V C H O P I N S
C F H A M M E R S E R O C S
X B L P I A N O F O R T E O
```

Solution on Page 350

APARTMENT

ASYLUM

BARN

BASEMENT

BOX

BRIDGE

BUS STOP

CAR

CONDO

COTTAGE

COVER

FORT

GARAGE

HOME

HOOD

HOSPITAL

HOTEL

HOUSE

HUT

IGLOO

INN

MANSION

MOTEL

OFFICE

OVERHANG

PATIO

PAVILION

REFUGE

ROOF

SHACK

SHED

TARP

TENT

TRAILER

TREE

TUNNEL

UMBRELLA

VEHICLE

YURT

```
E H M S N X J A L V P S Y V
L O O H R W T N R E E R T R
A M X A A Y Z E L E T O H A
T E M C B R I D G E F O M C
I P G K V E H I C L E U M O
P A D A L L J X N V L K G V
S O P B R I O G Q Y S D X E
O D T A Q A P N S T R U Y R
H N U S R R G A R J M M E O
O O N E S T W H V B O A C O
U C N M F U M R R I O N I F
S D E E O T B E T Z L S F L
E D L N I H L V N T G I F B
X O B T T L V O E T I O O N
C O T T A G E F T Q U N R N
S H E D P R A T V V Y H T I
```

Solution on Page 351

ABDOMEN

APPENDIX

ARM

BLADDER

BLOOD

BONE

BRAIN

CELLS

DIGESTIVE

DISSECTION

ELBOW

EYE

FEET

FIBULA

FINGER

FOOT

GLANDS

HAND

HEAD

INTESTINES

JOINTS

KNEE

LEG

LIMBS

LIVER

LUNG

MOUTH

NECK

NERVES

NOSE

ORGAN

SKIN

SKULL

SPINE

TEETH

THROAT

TIBIA

TISSUE

TOE

WRIST

```
Y B V C A F H E A D U I P G
U W X D O A N R E G N I F B
R R M O N L P A J Q N N R U
O I T D K U N P G T E A Q T
U S A E C B Z U E R I R S A
K T P D E I D S V N O M B O
N S K I N F T E I S D D I R
F L E S N I S G T B O I E H
Y Y U S N E X L S M L V X T
R C S E B H S A E I I R B E
T P S C O T A N G L E T E E
F O I T N U S D I D L N L T
E O T I E O J S D E K U I N
B L O O D M G A Y M N B K O
B J A N S L L E C G I S M S
T E Z W O B L E L A P D Z E
```

Solution on Page 351

Spring Is Here

Queen Bee

Lightweight Things

First Aid

Printing Press

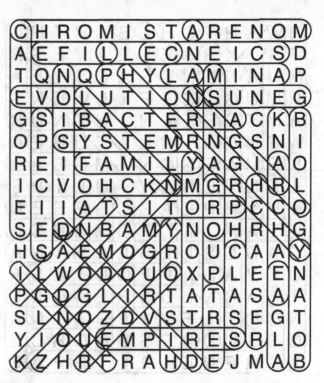

Biology Kingdom

Heavy Things

Bald Eagle

316

Descriptions

Easter Bunny

Champagne

Ends with an _L_

At the YMCA

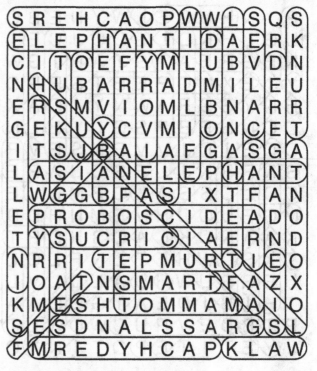

Giant Elephants

At a Planetarium

The Media

318

Homecoming

Vinegar

Creativity

Paintball Fun

Polo Shirt

```
O Z G C M S F H T O L C A W
T U A K O G O L A C O S T E
E N S A J S P O R T S N H K
K I R S I N N E T S T Y L E
C F O E M B R O I D E R E D
O O L J E A N S C C C A T N
P R O F E S S I O N A L I A
R M C L N V S M Y L S P C R
E W T O L S F B S S U H H B
P S E G A O L U L H A L P H
P L K L R E O T A I L A C Y
Y E C T M V O T C R N U Z F
N E A B Y Y S O K T W R F T
O V L E X P E N S I V E I O
P E P C B V D E S I G N T K
M W S T Q C N M T D K E L S
```

Boardwalk

```
O R I V E R W A L K W A Y U
C S T N O R F R E T A W P S
E D S L E T O H E R O O E T
A G N I H S I F H E C E O R
N B E A C H E S W S E D P O
F O O D L N U F S T A I L L
R P E D E S T R I A N S E L
O P I Z Z A I E R U C A X I
N S K C A N S Y R R I E P N
T S A O C T S A E A T S E G
Y L S K N A L P F N Y K N A
E Y D N A C N O T T O C S M
N I C E C R E A M S S C I E
S T S I R U O T R E I P V S
I W E I V Z F A M I L I E S
D L A V I N R A C R I D E S
```

Starts with a *C*

```
H O T V I T N M C E T N I Y
O Q R U Y A P U S L C F G L
H P A L C T B J L B U D R Q
Z J I C K B R A C F H R X M
W P O H C A U O C C P D F I
M I S I C C T L X V I B E Z
L A F P S G I F C B U L A E
C A L M S P P T Z W Y Y I P
E M A C A M P S Y A V R H M
C G C W C S A A L O P U C T
R L I A C A I C Z T N R I X
Y X G L K A S R W H M F C D
B E G C E E V E K P Y O J T
N L A D P C H E U G A H A G
R T O I A C H I N L F O V P
H C O P A C T C W O C A M B
```

Around Alaska

```
R I D E N A L I J U N E A U
E B S O M O O S E W A R D F
C A N A D A N O K U Y F G R
I R C D F R E E Z I N G N O
G R A S R E I C A L G O I Z
D O R A T I D I T S A V T E
R W I W U T N M F N R E N N
C E B E N N N U A I G R U O
P F O A D O O E I A N H M E
R I U T R R R L R T I M N E
E L P H A F T O B N H E O E
T D S E I D H R A U S N M S
N L B R L C E T N O I T L I
I I N O N I R E K M F T A U
W W C A Z S N P S W O N S R
L I O M I K S E T A M I L C
```

Energy Everywhere

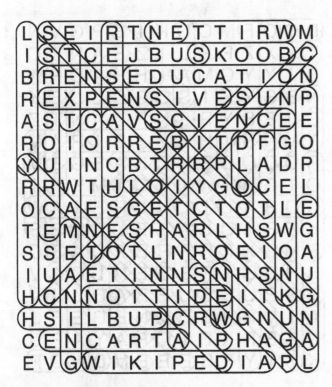

Encyclopedias

Ice Age

Axe

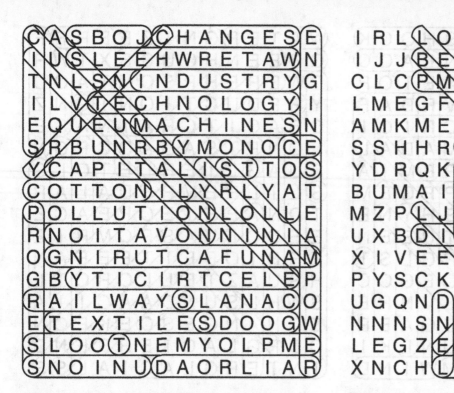

The Industrial Revolution

Starts with an *L*

Wave Action

Pet Fish

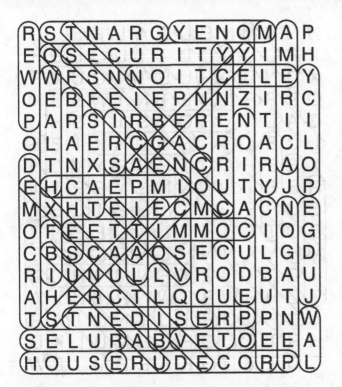

The Federal Government

Ballpoint Pen

Ends with an *H*

Interchange

Three-*S* Words

Log Cabin

Blue Things

Movie Projector

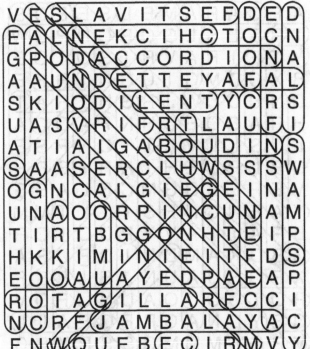

Cajun Life

Electronic Game

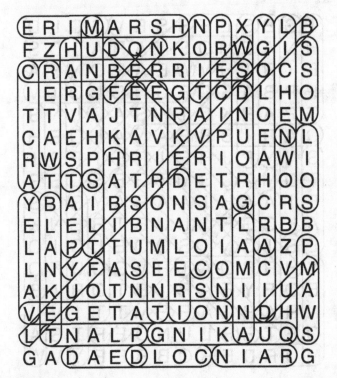

Bog

Types of Chocolate

HE Words

Apples to Apples

Visit Hong Kong

Watch Out for Pirates

Dream It

See a Ghost

Roses for You

Starts with a V

Slot Machine

Drive a Ferrari

Plastic Please

Bird Watcher

328

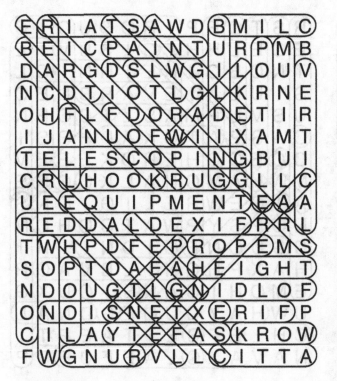

Ladder

Dump Trucks

Time to Cook

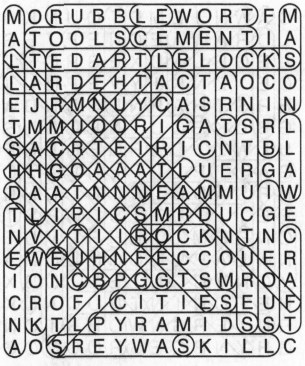

Stonemasonry

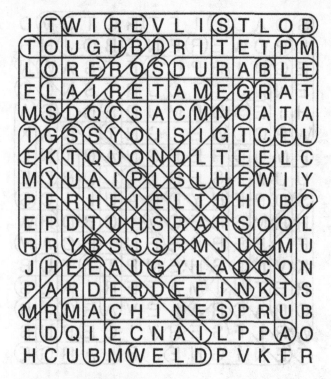

Strong Steel

Native Americans

Horse Show

See the Lighthouse

Ladder

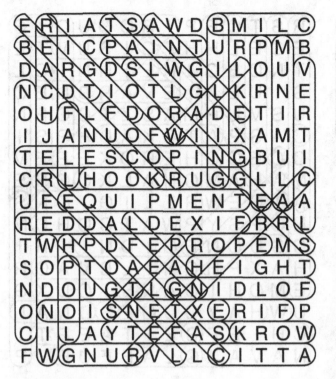

Dump Trucks

Time to Cook

Stonemasonry

Strong Steel

Native Americans

Horse Show

See the Lighthouse

330

Cheap Things

Around the Midwest

Dark Things

Bicycle Tire

Join the Navy

Quick Words

Bright Things

The World of Star Trek

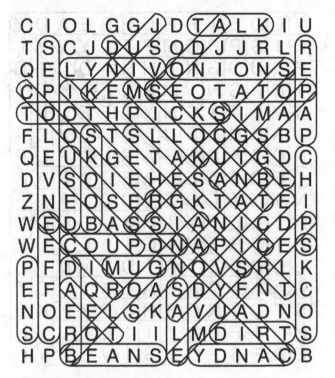

Cheap Things

Around the Midwest

Dark Things

Bicycle Tire

Join the Navy

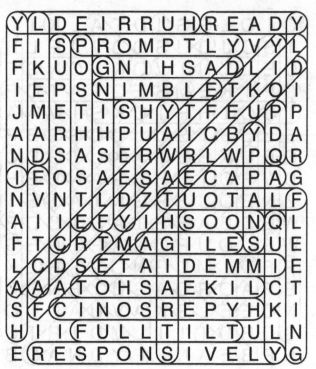

Quick Words

Bright Things

The World of Star Trek

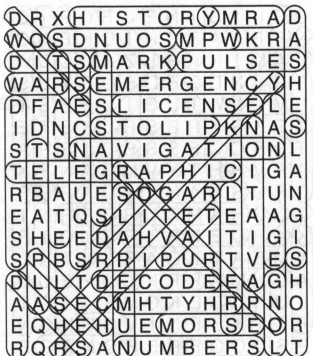

Morse Code Message

Julia Child

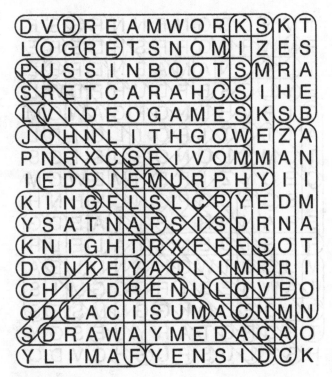

Shrek

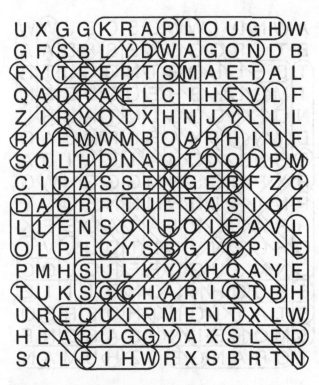

Horse-Drawn Vehicle

Around the Sahara

On Fire

Beefy

Lawn Mower

All Aboard Amtrak

Theater of the United States

Jimi Hendrix

Zebras Are Cool

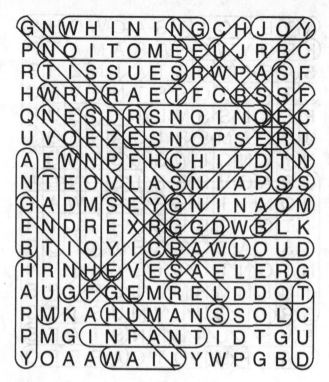

Crying

Toyota

US Words

Reggae Music

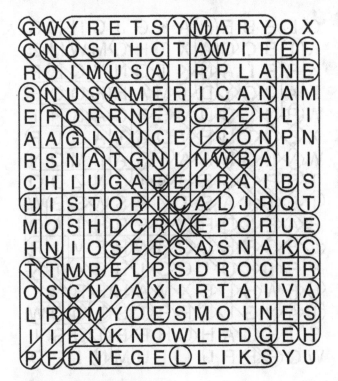

Amelia Earhart

Hand Pump

Tails

Oak

Trip to Maine

Fishnet

TT **Words**

Martin Luther King

338

Sack of Potatoes

Sound

Nonverbal Communication

Welding Together

Starts with an N

Game of Tag

Summer Camp Fun

Starts with a P

Greeting Cards

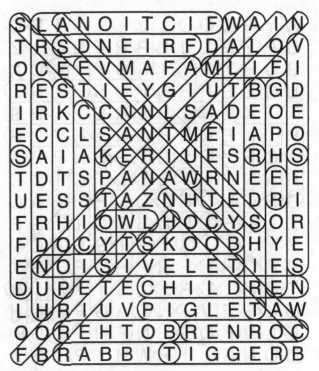

Winnie the Pooh

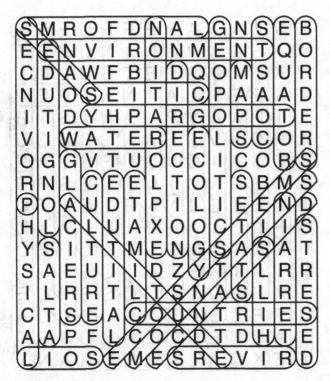

Geography

Pablo Picasso

```
W Y G Q O Q L J E T T I R D
U F Y P L J L R R F N Q I Z
B D H T F T I S S P I H D X
U G Z E R H H P U S H I N G
T I K E N I H S R E V I H S
H I K E N R H G N I H S U R
I Q F Y O S Q T H P N P P S
R A N I H T B S L T C I Z Q
D P C U S H I O N P H F A Q
X L H H L H D B O C I I S B
X Y I T I S I S I S E A C N
T R C H H E R P H H F T H K
T G K I C R V I S I X H I M
O J E E V I N E A G F E N H
E L N F Q G H N F H P T D W
D O N E L I H W H I P I B A
```

HI **Words**

```
T E K C I R C Y N I M I J Y
P T L P I N O C C H I O C A
U T I A E S D M T G S D H L
P E T T T S S I O A C O I P
P N E R A Y O A S V H N L N
E O R R E L R N L N I K D O
T I A F E H I I G C E E R S
S R T A T V T A A N V Y E E
M A U N O S R A N F O R N G
A M R T Y R I A F E U L B R
E R E A L B O Y C T S T O O
R M U S I C A L N D S H O W
D A F Y O B N E D O O W K S
D G T W N O V E L B U O R T
L I E S S D N E I R F G W H
O C Y N A N I M A T I O N R
```

Pinocchio

```
H S T V J P H H K W X A E V
Q G K E N S E A W F S L N C
O E D L E I F O Y K K T U R
F U E R T O R D S C Y T H E
Y E H Z O K G E I U C H F L
V T N D I V D S A L O G U D
L G N I N A E L G P R E R A
E A K E B N M S B I N D E R
L A G P M M H O V I G D H C
X F B R T E O H H W A R T S
P M A G A R L C H O Z N A Q
K F D V K I A P O M M O G P
Q L E D E M N C M U G S O D
V S A O W H E A T I S R R T
P R T T O O L U X O C E I D
K R H L S D A C N V R P U M
```

Reaper

```
R V I N T A G E F R U I T S
X A H D Q P G N I N U R P E
J K G A B S R E T S U L C L
E N P E R L A I N N E R E P
L I R W N V P L A N T S T R
L R E V V I E A N G D N C U
Y D S A I C V S U E S I A P
S O S R N D I M T N E S R R
E O E I E J N N R I E I T O
N F C E Y A E B I D D A X D
I N N T A M E U T A L R E U
W I A I R S R N I C E H S C
H K R E D I G C O S S V O E
I S F S S F P H N U S L U A
T A B L E N O E R M O S R T
E F K C A L B C U R R A N T
```

Great Grapes

Ethical

Bow

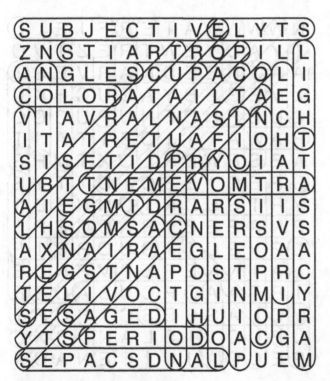

Impressionists

Starts with an *R*

Coffee Roasting

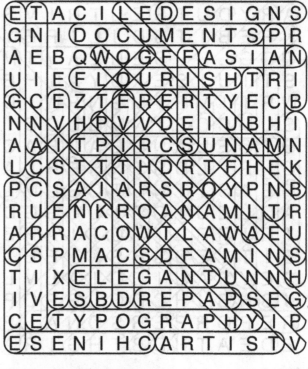

Fancy Writing

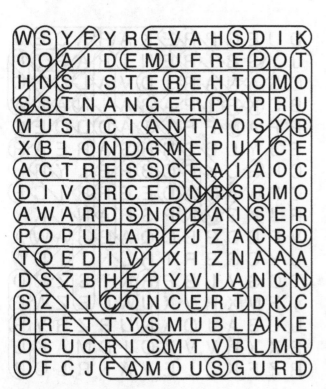

Britney Spears

Sugarcane

Simple Machines

Go Ice Skating

Drinking Straw

What Knot

Window

Sailing Mast

Sugary Sweet

Mary Poppins

Dig Archaeology

Starts with a G

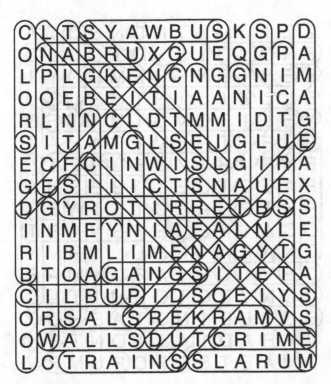

Graffiti

Footwear

Michael Jackson

Punk Rock Music

Angelic

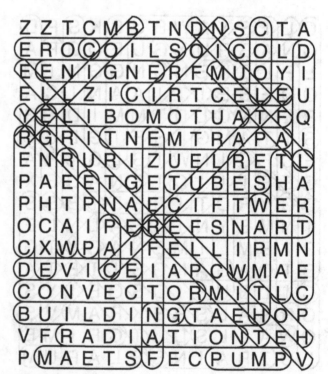

Radiator

348

Blogging

Parrots

Sharks All Around

Educating

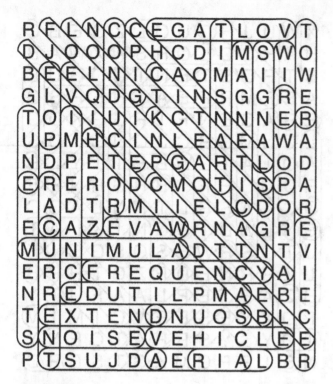

Antenna

OO Words

Snakes Alive!

Perfect Pianos

350

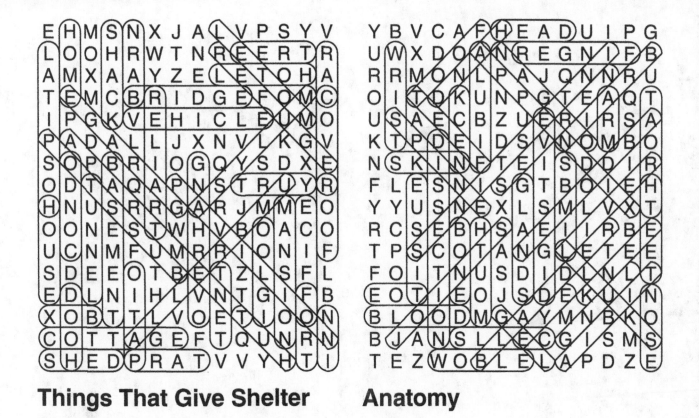

Things That Give Shelter **Anatomy**